FEATURED TEACHERS

8 — Caitlyn Giff

A Teacher Surfer's Guide to Adventures for the Mind, Body, and Soul

96 — Carmen Myer

How to Style It: Teacher Fashion Tips

84 — Janice Wan

Getting Started with Organic Soap Making

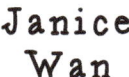

90 — Michaela Backlund

Abundance Through Simplicity: How Minimalism Can Lead to Finding Gratitude

24 — Tiffaney Whyte

Teach One; Impact Many

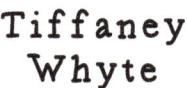

68 — Olivia Rose Martins

Empowering Students with Disabilities by Creatively Bridging the Employment Gap

gratitude is the fairest blossom which springs from the soul >> henry ward beecher

CONTENTS

remember when you wished for what you have right now?

The Impact of Drawing on Memory	18
Tips for Teaching Twins	20
10 Things to Do While Monitoring a Test	30
Vitamins Teachers Need Most	32
Cultivating Ownership to Combat Entitlement	42
Ways to Bust Out of a Creative Rut	46
Indicators of Deception: How to Spot a Lie	56
Teaching with Depression	64
A Positive Twist: Handle Common Challenges with a Spin	74
Creative Classroom Corners	78
Report Card Comments Made Easy	82
Your Guide to Classroom Parties	94
Growing in Gratitude	100
Bonus Templates to Copy	103

IN EVERY ISSUE

From the Editor	4
Bell Work	7
Classroom Tour	34
Discover	23
Passing Notes	54
Mind of a Creator	58
Inspiration From...	106

58

Mental Grounding Through Ceramics

48

Teaching Gratitude & Battling Entitlement

SNOWDAYMAGAZINE.COM | 3

FROM THE EDITOR...

You've probably already heard that practicing gratitude will lead you to happiness, but a spirit of grateful living is not always easy to achieve. That's because it's more complicated than it may appear. Brother David Steindl-Rast, a Benedictine monk, describes gratitude as having two main components. First, there is a sense of deep appreciation, since you acknowledge the value of what you have. Secondly, you recognize that the source of the gift is outside of yourself. It's freely given, either by God, or by other people. Depending on what blessing you are grateful for at the moment, you must accept that like a gift, it's not always earned. And like a gift, the value of any particular blessing hinges upon the perception of the recipient. **The amount of value you *imagine* accompanies each aspect of your life directly becomes the amount of happiness it will bring you.** As Brother David states, "Gratefulness is the key to a happy life that we hold in our hands."

The Latin root *gratus* means "pleasing" or "thankful." Unlike a feeling of indebtedness, the feeling of gratitude mustn't contain any pressure to pay back the favor. There is an aura of contentedness around the concept of gratitude. You don't have to do anything but continue on happily, acknowledging that you've got something good.

However, any time we can accompany an internal grateful feeling with an outward, physical reflection of that appreciation, we can help hardwire our brains for happiness. Tendencies toward a grateful attitude have been directly linked to happiness. Neuroscientists at the University of California discovered that when participants were given gifts, they had brain responses that showed lower stress levels, social rewards, and activation of the hypothalamus, which releases dopamine, the pleasure hormone. But they saw further neurological impacts when the participant then enhanced that feeling of gratitude by following it up with a written thank you note. By outwardly showing their gratitude, and reflecting on it with a written letter, the individuals showed a lasting impact, with long-term changes in the medial prefrontal cortex (which is a reward center of the brain that also is associated with social emotions, empathy, and value perception) three months later.

In adolescents, this long-lasting effect even offers a feeling of protection, and leads to lower bullying and suicide rates. Practicing gratitude and reflecting on it can aid teens in self-worth and biologically reprogram their brains to increase tendencies for happiness.

Practice appreciation, and teach it to your students. Don't discount the impact of writing in a gratitude journal, expressing verbal thanks, and reflecting on gift giving and receiving. Gratitude can be taught, and must be consistently worked toward. Gratitude is more than just an emotion. It's a choice.

Teaching a gratitude mindset may be even more imperative than teaching the more popular "growth mindset." If you teach gratitude, respect will flow from it. Empathy will flow from it. Happiness will flow from it. These are what we all really need, even more than we need success, knowledge, or educational growth. Growing in gratitude is one of the most critical forms of growth we can prioritize for ourselves and our students.

And remember, teaching gratitude is about modeling, not forcing.
Practice your own gratitude out loud.
They will copy.

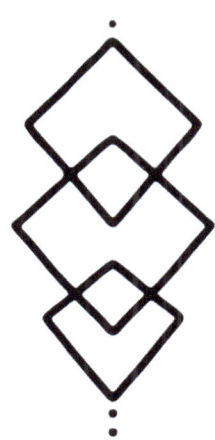

Let Snowday be your guide to a productive, thoughtful, passionate life as an educator AND as a creative, vibrant human soul!

- Brigid

SPOTLIGHT THEME IN THIS ISSUE:
"GROWING IN GRATITUDE"

It's a funny thing about life, once you begin to take note of the things you are grateful for, you begin to lose sight of the things that you lack.
>> Germany Kent

Editor & Publisher
Brigid Danziger

Editing & Proofreading
Michael Dober

Writers
Kelly Barendt
Brigid Danziger
Shannon Gareau
Brittany Naujok

Sponsored and Produced by
Math Giraffe, LLC

Follow On Instagram
@snowdaymagazine

Contact Us
editor@snowdaymagazine.com

Advertising
media@snowdaymagazine.com

Website
SNOWDAYMAGAZINE.COM

Copyright 2020

All rights reserved. Views, comments, and suggestions do not necessarily represent those of the publisher, and are provided as is. Snowday's editor and publisher disclaim any and all legal responsibility for the reader's use of any information included in this publication. Content given is not intended as a replacement for consulting an expert.

No portion of this publication may be reproduced without permission.

BELL WORK

This time, the bell work is in the self-care realm, just for YOU!

Objective:
Create a DIY face scrub with ingredients from your kitchen that will soothe and nourish your skin while energizing you each morning.

1. EXFOLIANT:
Choose a base that will bring the grit. Use sugar, brown sugar, or coffee grounds. Put 1 cup of your exfoliating base in a small bowl.

2. OIL:
Add a nourishing oil for moisture. About 1/3 cup of coconut oil is usually perfect, but you can adjust the measurements based on how thick you prefer your scrub to be.

3. SCENT:
Throw in a few drops of peppermint essential oil, a sprinkling of your favorite herbs, or a touch of citrus zest to bring life to your scrub and energize you when you wash your face.

4. BOOSTERS:
If you need any extra ingredients, now is the time to add them! Blueberries, for example, are loaded with antioxidants and Vitamin C, making them a really healthy skin booster for those with acne. Honey can soften and smooth skin, while green tea can tighten up loose skin or help decrease the appearance of scars.

Mix well, then use your scrub each day, watching for any allergies, and avoiding broken skin.

ADVENTURES FOR THE *mind*
ADVENTURES FOR THE *body*
ADVENTURES FOR THE *soul*

STRATEGIES FOR LIVING
A WELL-ROUNDED LIFE
WITH SURFER & TEACHER
CAITLYN GIFF

@surfingiff
- *teacher*
- *painter*
- *musician*
- *vegetarian*

Most people don't realize that surfing life happens all over the world, even in places that are thousands of miles from the nearest ocean. I've surfed in the middle of the desert in the UAE, and in the surfing community here in Toronto. When I tell people that I'm excited to try lake surfing on Lake Ontario, they look at me like I have three heads. There is a growing and committed surf community in Toronto who surf on the Great Lakes whenever there is swell. Surfers are so committed (or addicted rather), that they will try to find a wave to surf pretty much anywhere.

I've surfed in February in Australia, Halifax, and Dubai, and I plan to do the same in Ontario this year. So yes, you would be surprised at the places you can find waves to surf.

I'm a small town girl who always had dreams of seeing the world. I grew up on a hobby farm near Athens, Ontario. I loved playing outside with my siblings and hunting deer and turkey with my dad. I really enjoyed my childhood, but I always dreamed of living in far away places and seeing what was beyond my own reality.

When I was going to the University of Ottawa, there was an opportunity to go to Australia on an exchange. To go, you had to have a grade point average of 4.0. I, like many young students, had a very fun first year but wasn't as productive with my education as I could have been. Due to my extra curricular activities in the first year, my GPA was nowhere near a 4.0. I really wanted to go on the exchange, so I worked hard that year. Really hard. I got really good grades, and when it was time to submit all my references and paperwork, they told me I only had a GPA of 3.9 and couldn't go.

I was devastated. Later that week I was walking home from class in the dead of winter. There was ice all over, but something sparkling on the road caught my eye. I walked over, bent down, and picked up a small necklace charm. To my shock and amazement, I was holding a tiny Australian Emblem. I knew then and there that my dream was still alive and it would happen one day.

After University, I was living at home and had no idea what I wanted to do with my life. I was working as a bartender at a local bar in my hometown. One day, my old high-school drama teacher, Mr. Mcneil, was sitting at the bar enjoying a pint. I was telling him I wasn't sure what I wanted to do with my life but I had been volunteering at a daycare and liked working with kids. The words that would change my life forever came out of his mouth: "Caitlyn, did you know you can go to Teachers' College in Australia and then come back to Canada and work as a teacher?" That night, I raced home and applied to several schools in Australia. Within a few months, I was

> I walked over, bent down, and picked up a small necklace charm. To my shock and amazement, I was holding a tiny Australian Emblem. I knew then and there that my dream was still alive and it would happen one day.

on a plane making my dream of living in a far away land a reality. From that time, I've learned to surf, sail, and play guitar. I've traveled to extraordinary places, and met some amazing humans that shaped who I am today.

I am now an elementary school teacher with a background in psychology. I got my graduate diploma in education at the University of the Sunshine Coast in Australia. I did my undergrad at Ottawa University. I've taught in Australia, Halifax and recently in the Middle East. Currently, I have taken a role at a private school in Toronto that is outside of the classroom but still working directly with students. I am the After Care and Fun Plus coordinator. I coordinate the after school care as well as the after school programming and activities for grades K-6. This is an awesome job as I get to interact with kids in a fun and relaxed setting while coordinating interesting and impactful after school activities.

Time for Personal Passions on Teaching Days
I'm a busy body by nature, so it suits me well to be busy with lots of hobbies and activities. I stay busy surfing, painting, playing guitar, meeting up with friends, and helping my partner with his business. Recently, I took up rock climbing. I love all these activities, but surfing is my passion. Growing up in a small town in rural Ontario, I never dreamed that I would become a surfer. Soon after moving to Australia I went on a surf retreat, and after that trip I was completely head over heels hooked on surfing. I've surfed for 8 years now, and am always looking for opportunities to get in the water and ride waves.

Teaching allows me to travel to amazing surf destinations around the world, so I've had the pleasure of surfing in places like the Philippines, New Zealand, Sri Lanka, and Costa Rica, to name a few. My apartment in Australia was practically on the beach. Each morning I would get up super early to surf before work and then usually after work on my way home I would stop and jump into the water for a session before dinner. It was the best stress reliever I've ever found in my teaching career, which came in handy as a new teacher.

When I decided to move back to Canada, I made the decision to move to the East Coast so I could still be near the Ocean. I settled on Halifax which was only a 35 minute drive to the

ocean. If I ever finished work early I would rush to the beach to get a surf in after work, and of course spent most weekends at the beach. The best surfing in Halifax is in the winter, which didn't really bother me except I always wanted to stay out longer. My body would tell me otherwise, and I'd be forced to get out shivering and nearly blue.

When I lived in the Middle East, I still managed to find surf. In the desert I found a man-made wave pool in Al Ain that I would frequent. I also kept an eye on the weather and would drive to Dubai (an hour from where I lived) whenever there looked like there might be waves. The trick was knowing how to read the weather charts, which I got pretty good at. I also had the luxury of making a good income there and could fly to some amazing surf destinations from Dubai. Now that I live in Toronto I plan to lake surf and travel in the summer and over longer breaks. Right now I'm waiting for my surfboards to arrive from overseas so I can try surfing on Lake Ontario. This summer, my partner and I are planning a trip to California where we can surf and rock climb together.

Balancing the Priorities Strategically

The strategies that help me find time to surf include scheduling my time and working smart. I use google calendars religiously. If it's in my calendar, I'm more likely to get it done. Teacher life is extremely busy and things come up all the time, so being extra organized with my time allows me to schedule time for myself. I also am the type of person who doesn't bring work home with me. At the beginning of my career I would always bring work home, which meant I would be working into the evening and had little time for myself.

I've learned that in order to have a healthy work/life balance you need to leave it at the door when you leave. This also means you need to work smart while at work. If I have any free time, even 5 minutes, I complete a task that needs to be done. I don't waste time at work so I have more free time after work for myself.

I believe that nurturing your whole self (mind, body, and soul) is vital to longevity in any career, but especially in teaching. Teaching is physically and mentally exhausting. You need to find time to keep your mind and body healthy in order to survive a career of teaching. I schedule meditation into my daily routines at school. I teach the kids about meditation and its benefits, and we do it together. It's a great way to calm students down after recess.

As far as keeping my body healthy, I think my diet does this for me in big ways. Being a gluten free, dairy free vegetarian doesn't leave a whole lot on the menu that is bad for me. I'm not saying everyone should be eating this diet, but definitely be conscious about what you are putting into your body. Sugar is something I try desperately to avoid, especially during the day. Sugar will bring you up and then send you crashing down.

Physical activity for me is a huge stress reliever. I need it to keep my mind and body healthy. That being said, I hate going to the gym. The thought of going to a gym is not something that gets me excited. So rather than going to a gym I try to find physical activities that are enjoyable for me such as surfing, rock climbing, bicycle riding, hiking, etc. When the activity is fun it never feels like a 'work out.'

On weekends my partner and I try to be as active as possible. If the weather is good, we go outdoor climbing. If not, we hit up the climbing gym. We try to schedule time for family and friends too. I think it's also really important to find some down time during the weekend. We try to schedule at least one morning or one evening where we aren't committed to anything. This can be challenging sometimes, but when it happens we both really appreciate it. During those uncommitted times, we find ourselves making music, food, or just going for a stroll outside.

Meditative Creativity
Painting, for me, is meditation. I can lose myself in my painting for hours at a time. There is something about the colours and the intentional focus that allow my brain to really relax and forget about anything else that might be going on. I go through spurts with how much I am painting. Sometimes I will have a painting out on the table and work on it for weeks. Other times I put the paintings away and have a break for a while. I notice that when the weather gets bad and I'm inside for longer periods of time, that's when I paint the most.

I find inspiration in nature for my paintings. When I was living in the UAE I was really missing the ocean, so I decided to paint an underwater reef scene. If I am missing surfing, I'll find myself painting waves. If I am craving the woods, I'll paint trees. For me, it's not only a creative outlet, but another way to connect with nature.

My advice is to meditate and find time to do the things you love. Meditation has done wonders for my life. I think I would have had a nervous breakdown had I not found meditation. When I'm practicing meditation on a regular basis, I notice that my entire body feels lighter and the little things that normally get under my skin just don't seem that important.

When we meditate, it allows our brains to slow down and make room for things like creativity. Also, as I said before: schedule, schedule, schedule. It is so important to schedule time for ourselves. At the beginning of each week, find a time that can be all about you. Schedule it and stick to it. You will thank yourself later.

Getting Started with a New Passion
I think that we are all capable of doing pretty much anything, but there are several reasons we don't. The first thing that gets in our way is our fear or self doubt. In order to get started with something, you must first face your fear. Allow yourself to feel the fear, but do the thing that scares you anyways. Once you start on the path, the fear will become less and less.

The second thing that stops us from doing new things is time. Most people have way more time than they think they do. The reality is that we just don't manage our time well, or we don't know how to prioritize our time. Really examine how you spend your time. Do you spend a couple of hours a night watching Netflix like

> I believe that nurturing your whole self (mind, body, and soul) is vital to longevity in any career, but especially in teaching.

most of us do? Could some of that time be devoted to learning something new?

The last thing that gets in our own way is a lack of energy. This is a big one, because energy is essential to getting motivated to do pretty much anything. This is why we must create healthy habits such as getting enough sleep and eating the right food. These two things alone will help to boost energy levels.

One example is how I learned to play the guitar. I wanted to learn to play guitar, but I thought I was too old and my hands were to small to learn to play. (This was my fear.) I bought a guitar anyways and asked a friend to show me some basics. From there, I decided to pick the guitar up every day for at least 5 minutes. By doing this, little by little I saw improvements. Now I can play the guitar. I'm no Jimi Hendrix, but I can play a handful of songs quite well and I will continue to practice to learn more.

Don't forget that effort is everything, and some things, like playing guitar or learning to surf, can take years. That's ok, though. You will appreciate and value the skill that much more when you work hard for it.

Issues and Impact in Education
I recently moved to Toronto. During my flight back to Canada, the Ontario government announced there would be significant cuts to funding for the public education system. Luckily, I had already secured a job at a private school. I can't really speak for the public school system here, but the school I work at is wonderful. I know that I am privileged to work there. I know that most schools in the public school system don't get anywhere near the amount of funding we do. I have to remind myself of that every day in order to stay humble in my current job.

I'm fortunate enough to work at a school that follows the Reggio Emilia approach. One of the key pillars of this approach is the importance of nature. Being in nature is so important for me. Being surrounded by nature brings a sense of peace over me. In the Middle East, there were few opportunities to be in nature. I really noticed a difference in my overall mood. When I would travel to surf destinations and suddenly be surrounded by trees, grass, and ocean, I would feel an instant boost in my mood and attitude. I think nature is vital to living a balanced life. Even taking a walk outside while looking up at the trees can lower your stress levels.

We take the students to a ravine close to our school once every 8 days, just to be in nature. We also have a strict policy for recess. No extra curricular activities are to be done during 'DEAP' time (drop everything and play). We feel as though being outside is so important for human development. Our school has also brought many natural elements into the school. Instead of counting plastic cubes for math, the students count rocks or pine cones. In every classroom you will find living plants, tree limbs, shells, etc. Visitors to our school always comment on the serenity they feel walking through the school, and I believe it has a lot to do with how we have invited nature indoors.

A Nurturing Atmosphere
My own environment has the ability to impact me in good or bad ways, depending on the environment. It is important for work and home environments to be clean and organized. When my home or work environment is cluttered, my brain feels cluttered. I feel better when everything has a 'home.' I work hard to teach the kids in my class where everything goes and encourage them to put things back in their 'home.'

I also think lighting is really important for my environment. At work, I prefer a classroom with a lot of natural light. This will help keep the students and teacher alert. Plants are also essential in my home and classroom. Plants help clean the air and help to lower stress levels. All these things create a calm and peaceful environment.

We are responsible for shaping the minds of generations to come. Our own future depends on the minds we are impacting today. The environment as we know it is crumbling at alarming rates. It is our job to help children see the value in the environment. We must make choices in our classroom that will show students we can all make a difference, provide opportunities, and guide and nurture students' curiosity and natural empathy towards the environment. We need more people who care so that there will be a future to care about.

Caitlyn's Tips

Favorite Teacher Hack:
I have a "picking pot." At the beginning of the year I write each student's name on a popsicle stick. The sticks go into a jar and I use the picking pot for choosing random groups, games, for picking helpers, or for asking students questions. It's definitely a must have in my class. The picking pot is fair, and children can't argue with the picking pot because it's random.

Favorite Life Hack:
I love having ready-to-eat food for breakfast for those busy mornings. I can't eat dairy or gluten and I'm vegetarian (yeah, I'm *that* person at dinner). Food can sometimes be a challenge for me. I recently discovered chia seed pudding. You can make it in a mason jar the night before, and it's super easy to make. It's 1 part chia seeds to 3 parts almond milk (or any type of milk you like). You can add whatever flavours you like. I really love adding a heaping spoon of natural peanut butter and a dash of maple syrup. In the morning you will have a healthy, delicious breakfast on the go!

Morning Routine:
I am not a morning person, so I usually take about 3 or 4 snoozes before I can get out of bed. Once I am up, I make my way to the bathroom, where I wake myself up fully with a shower. After my shower, I meditate for 5-10 minutes, depending on time. After this, I start work on the business I am helping my boyfriend with, *Deep Work Sprints*. After working on this for about an hour, I eat breakfast. Sometimes I cook some eggs and fried tomatoes, but if I'm short on time, I have something simple like gluten free toast and natural peanut butter or chia seed pudding. After I eat, I get dressed and ready for work and make my way to the subway.

Teaching Advice:
I have two pieces that have really resonated with me over my teaching career.
1. "There is something special and loveable in every single child. We only need to take a moment to find it." >> Mrs. Carol Smith
2. "Words should not be used as a shortcut to knowledge." >> Loris Malaguzzi

Music Recommendations:
I am a big fan of folk alternative like *The Lumineers* or *Mumford and Sons*. I also have an ongoing playlist that I keep adding to called 'New Music I like' which anyone can find if they search me on Spotify. My Spotify name is Caitlyn Suzanne. Check it out and if you know a song I might like, send me a message on Instagram. I'm always looking for new music.

Q&A with Caitlyn

How would you describe your own style?
My style is very much Canadian surf chick. I love plaid. I love army green. I love big brown boots with a dress. Now that I am living in Canada, I mix my beach style with a pair of big brown lace up boots and thick black tights. I'm not interested in spending my month's salary on clothes, so a couple of times a year I go to second hand stores and spend hours going through the clothes. You would be surprised what you can find, and for a fraction of the cost. It's good for my bank account and for the environment!

What is your favorite lunch to pack for school?
I love to cook. I also love leftovers for lunch. So for lunch it wouldn't be surprising for you to see me eating anything from vegetarian pad Thai to a home made bean chilli.

What are you most grateful for?
I am most grateful for my health. I am a healthy woman who is able to do the things she loves.

What fuels your soul?
If you asked me this question 3 years ago, I would have said surfing. But now I'm an aunt to 3 nieces. They are a big reason I moved back to Canada. I get this overwhelming feeling of happiness when I'm with them. They're now at the age that they know me. When they see me, they shout my name and excitedly run over to hug me hello. That is the feeling that fills my soul. I can't even imagine what it will be like when I have my own kids!

Can you share 5 tips for something important to you?
5 tips for being beautiful:
1. Smile
2. Be kind
3. Be humble
4. Say hello
5. Be grateful

Tell us about one last thing you'd love to share:
I would love to share what I have been working on in the mornings with my partner. We are starting a business called "Deep Work Sprints". Deep Work Sprints is an online co-working community where entrepreneurs and remote workers can get their deepest work done. It's an accelerator for reaching goals. I believe this online space could be useful for students as well.

Once we get the business going, I want to open a sprint specifically designed for students who work remotely or even are completing independent projects at school. It will be a space for them to have community, to bounce ideas off of other students from around the world, and be held accountable for accomplishing their tasks. The future is moving online, and my partner and I see great potential with this business. If you are interested in learning more, please feel free to reach out to me. I'd be happy to chat more about what we are doing.

Find Caitlyn on Instagram @surfingiff

Most people have way more time than they think they do. The reality is that we just don't manage our time well, or we don't know how to prioritize our time.

The Impact of Drawing on Memory

Sketching and drawing may not be common practices in your classroom, especially if you teach something like Math, Spanish, or Writing. But you may be missing out on a tool that would really enhance your assortment of teaching tricks. Drawing has been found to improve memory significantly better than other strategies, like writing, reading, or visualization.

In fact, drawing a picture will nearly double the retention of the lesson content. Researchers from the University of Waterloo conducted studies to explore whether drawing to-be-learned information enhanced memory and found it to be a reliable, replicable means of boosting performance.

What is the Research Behind This?

There were three main researchers conducting these studies: Myra A. Fernandes, Jeffrey D. Wammes, and Melissa E. Meade. They conducted a series of studies where they asked both young people and older adults to do a variety of memory-encoding techniques. Then, they tested their recall.

Edutopia explains one of their first experiments. "They asked undergraduate students to study lists of common terms—words like truck and pear—and then either write down or illustrate those words. Shortly afterward, participants recalled 20 percent of words they had written down, but more than twice as many—45 percent—of the terms they had drawn."

Later, they compared note-taking by writing down words and illustrating concepts with undergraduate students. The researchers found drawing to be "an effective and reliable encoding strategy, far superior to writing." (Sage Journals)

Why is Drawing Such a Powerful Memory Tool?

The results of these studies have shown us drawing is a powerful memory tool. So, now the question is … why?

The researchers of these studies propose that "drawing improves memory by promoting the integration of elaborative, pictorial, and motor codes, facilitating creation of a context-rich representation." (Sage Journals)

When you draw a picture, you force your brain to make connections with the term you are drawing. You elaborate on the given concept or term, which helps encode it into your memory.

"At a neural level, the strength of a memory depends largely on how many connections are made to other memories. An isolated piece of information—such as a trivial fact—is soon forgotten in the brain's constant effort to prune away unused knowledge. The opposite, however, is also true: The more synaptic connections a memory has, the more it resists eventually being forgotten." (Edutopia)

When a person draws a new piece of information, not only is he or she forming a motor connection with the hand-to-paper connection, but also deep synaptic connections.

Here's the best part- it doesn't matter how good you are at drawing! Artistic ability makes no difference in this powerful memory tool.

How Can You Incorporate Drawing in your Lessons?

Posters
Whether you're introducing a new topic, getting some extra practice, or reviewing for a test, divide your class into small groups and have them create and decorate a poster or an infographic on the topic to hang on the wall. Be sure they include plenty of pictures! Or if you're strictly working on key terms, have your students create a word wall including pictures!

Pictionary-like Game
A favorite game in many households can be adjusted to fit into your classroom! Divide your class into teams of 4 or 5. Write down vocabulary words or phrases on cards. Have each team send up their first artist to you to show the first card. Start a 60 second timer when they are ready to go! Walk around the room and listen for the first team to guess the word. The first team to say it gets a point on the board.

Visual Vocabulary
When students connect imagery with a key term, they build a mental memory trigger that will remind them of the meaning of the word. Develop these cues by having students sketch a graphic that is somehow representative of part of the concept. Award bonus points if they can embed the word in their graphic with cool lettering that integrates with their picture like a logo.

Sketching & Doodling
Even mindless doodles help students focus during a lecture, believe it or not! Allow kids to sketch alongside notes, or doodle in the margins to help their brains make connections as they listen.

Graphic Organizers
Amp up your graphic organizer game with pictoral charts, timelines, doodle organizers, and flow charts instead of (or in addition to) text based ones. Instead of writing inside each compartment on an organizer, students can draw or doodle icons that show ideas even more clearly.

tips for TEACHING TWINS

More sets of twins than ever are entering our classrooms. If you've never had a pair of siblings in your class at the same time before, you're likely to in the next few years. Here's what you'll need to know.

Why Twins Are on the Rise
Between 1980 and 2007, the number of twin births more than doubled in the United States. Twin birth rates hit a record high in 2014, according to the CDC. There were 33.9 twins born for every 1,000 births, compared to only 18.9 per 1,000 in 1980. Researchers have attributed the drastic changes to a few key factors.

A study in 2012 found that maternal age contributes to the increase. The largest change occured in women over the age of 30. Twin births used to occur most often for mothers between 35 and 39 years of age. However, now mothers 40 or older have even higher rates. 7% of deliveries for women in the 40+ age bracket were twins. As maternal age increases, more and more women are in this age bracket when they deliver, so their odds of multiples increase. Researchers found that the age factor accounts for a third of the rise in twin births.

Another study found that rising obesity rates may be contributing to the rising twin rates. Women who were tall or overweight were found to be more likely to deliver twins. The majority of the increase in twin births, however, can be attributed to fertility treatments. As reproductive assistance becomes more mainstream, the chances of conceiving multiples increases. This may also play a role in the fact that maternal age is correlated to twin births as well, since women over 30 are more likely to be receiving fertility assistance.

Since 2018, twin delivery rates are starting to drop back down slightly. As fertility treatments progress, the peak may now have passed. However, students born during those peak years are starting their school careers now, so expect at least a few more years with plenty of twins.

How to Help Your Twin Students Thrive
A variety of issues can arise when siblings are in the same grade. One of the biggest decisions to be made is whether or not they are placed in the same classroom, but this is less likely to come down to a teacher's decision these days. Many schools now have policies for how to deal with classroom assignments for twins, and 14 states have now even enacted twin laws. For example, Texas House Bill 314 lays out a system for parents to request placements for their multiple birth siblings and make the initial decision. It leaves room to reassess after the first grading period, gives some power to the principal, and allows for an appeal process for the parents.

Some schools may not run into this, if they have only one teacher per grade level, but if the issue arises, parents generally have some say, and principals usually have procedures to follow. Challenges that arise on the teacher level are generally more targeted toward the individuality of the children.

Whether or not twins are in the same classroom, the goal is always to ensure that each individual student is given the opportunity to thrive and maintain his or her own unique personality, intellect, and soul. Even with this understanding, teachers may fall into habits that they don't think twice about. Consider the following tips to avoid accidentally comparing siblings or devaluing their individuality.

Togetherness Balanced with Separation
Be extra aware of seating plans. You've probably already considered the fact that seating students alphabetically can put kids beside the same classmates across different periods throughout the day, or across different years. But with twins, this effect is doubled, because they are also together at home. Keep small details like this in mind when assigning seats or lockers.

Individuality & Identity
Never refer to two students as one entity. Avoid calling out groups with words like "Kelly, Edward,

and the twins." Use their names in exactly the same way that you would for all the rest of your students. Subtle details, like the way you refer to them and respect their individuality are easily overlooked by many people, but will not go unnoticed.

Your students will greatly appreciate every effort to get their names right. Never let on that you cannot tell two children apart. Prioritize getting to know who is who, and be very careful that you never joke about the fact that you can't tell the difference. It is your responsibility to know who each child in your care is, even in situations where it's more difficult to learn a name. Just because it is hard to differentiate between two people does not excuse you from doing your best to get it right. Neither the students nor the parents think it's comical that you can't get this straight. Ask for hints from other teachers on how to tell them apart if you really need to, but don't just give up.

Equity Does Not Mean Replication
However, it is not your responsibility to provide exactly the same learning experience for each twin. Just as you'd differentiate for two unrelated siblings, feel free to vary things based on individual needs. Do not feel required to replicate every special situation to fit the other twin. If one earns a reward, don't sit around wondering if you can offer it without giving the other sibling an opportunity. If you wouldn't think twice about it for any other two students in your class, you do not need to overdose on fairness for twins.

Heads Up About DNA
Identical twins may indeed have a lot in common as far as personality as well as physical looks. This is because they have matching DNA. Don't be alarmed if their work looks similar.

On the flip side, don't expect identical results, and be careful not to compare them to one another, especially aloud. Whether you have identical or fraternal twins, they may have very different strengths and challenges. Schedule their conferences at separate times, and compare each only to the expectation, not to the other. If the parents (or other students) do start bringing up sibling comparisons,

Sources: CDC, NY Times, TwinsMagazine.com

guide the conversation back where it needs to be.

Beware of Humor
Use caution when you think you're being funny or entertaining. Some teachers think a twin vs. twin competition is fun, or think nothing of playing around verbally with one twin or another about the differences between the two, in a playful or a competitive way. Put yourself in each one's shoes, not only the way you would for any student, but beyond that to consider whether your ideas or comments are inadvertently framing a child as half of an entity instead of a single, full person.

Not My Brother's Keeper
Don't take advantage of the fact that they love one another and live together. Their family bond does not mean that it's ok to make one student accountable for another. It seems obvious when dealing with most students that it is not a classmate's job to help anyone else to get organized, study, be on task, or remember homework. So apply that same concept to siblings. Each one is accountable only for him/herself.

What Twins and Their Parents Want You to Know

>> We are not an oddity for your entertainment. Don't ask weird questions or treat us differently, and have our backs if other kids do this. Ask us each in private how we want tricky situations handled.

>> It hurts our feelings and makes us feel less cared for when you brush off the fact that you can't tell us apart. You're sending a message that you don't care enough to know each of us, even if that is not your feeling or intent.

>> Don't compare us to one another. It's a no-win situation.

>> We want to be involved in the conversation and empowered to make choices. Your decisions impact us greatly.

>> Remember that we are two people, not just one pair.

Resources & Support

One and the Same: My Life as an Identical Twin and What I've Learned About Everyone's Struggle to Be Singular by Abigail Pogrebin shares her own experience as an identical twin and explores the nature of twin relationships. She helps parents (and teachers willing to go the extra mile to read) who wonder how to delicately balance the closeness with the separate individuality to best nurture twins.

No Two Alike, a children's book by Keith Baker features two birds. They explore branches, leaves, and snowflakes to discover that even things that look *almost* alike are each still unique. If you read this in class, be sure to have a private conversation with your twins to see what they are open to sharing with classmates during the class discussion about twins, individuality, and uniqueness. Ensure that everyone feels comfortable.

For more insight when problems arise, or to guide both teachers and parents, do a little research into Pat Preedy's three categories and assess the twins in your own care. Knowing whether they are "Extreme Individual," "Mature Dependent," or "Closely Coupled" may help you make decisions that will enhance their development.

DISCOVER soufuL homes

@LOVERENOVATIONS

Amanda is always up to something innovative, whether it's spicing up the back yard with major DIYs, choosing a paint color for her next front entryway project, or simply crafting a brand new wreath for the front door. She tells it exactly like it is and then blogs about it after. Follow along to see all her creative home renovation ideas that happen right alongside real day to day living as a mom of two boys.

@MISS_RUSTICARROW

As an incredibly creative soul and mom of twins, Nikki brightens up each morning for those who follow along with her crafty projects. She shares her unique design style while grinning her way through each day and enjoying life. Her positive spirit, passion for contrast and calming neutrals, and joy from each new rug she reveals is all just contagious! Whether she is singing to her boys or painting another "jaunt of a wall" you'd never expect, she and her beautiful family bring light and positivity to every single day.

OUR TOP PICKS FROM instagram FOR BEAUTY INSIDE AND OUT

We selected these trendy home influencers not only for their gorgeous designs, but also for their inspiring souls. These women know what's important and will offer you both home decor ideas as well as family values and genuine, relatable conversation.

@ARROWSANDBOW

Whether she is living in a trailer with three kids or renovating an enormous new house with a Beauty and the Beast style library wall (with a ladder and everything!), Ashley brings a smooth blend of competence and reality to every home project. She knows what life is all about, and keeps a beautiful balance of the true priorities. With faith, love, and plenty of dancing, she and her husband walk through each family challenge and each house challenge with grace. Follow their adventure, where they somehow make the ups, downs, and in betweens all into mountaintops in their life journey.

teach ONE... impact MANY

A student-oriented mentality is central to Tiffaney Whyte's teaching, but she also knows the value of supporting teachers, and prioritizes this with her creative business endeavors. We asked Tiffaney to share a bit about her adventures in education, give some creative insight, and offer a peek at how she balances teacher life with her own full life at home.

x x x x x x x x x x x x x x x x x x x x

SPECIAL EDUCATION TEACHER
T-SHIRT DESIGNER
CREATIVE SOUL

photography by Goody Bag Photography
https://bnj281.wixsite.com/goodphotography

"Special education is my sauce." This and a range of other fun phrases cover the fronts of the t-shirts in Tiffaney Whyte's teacher shop, De'AvionBlu Innovations. A quote close to her heart, "Teach one… impact many" is on a t-shirt, and even has a story behind it. Tiffaney is passionate about the fact that "you have the future in your classroom." This sentiment comes out not only on her designs, but also in the way that she treats her own students.

In her 5th grade classroom, Fridays are for self care, but not for the adults. You usually hear the term "self-care" in terms of teachers, moms, and professionals. This time, it's the students' turn. "My students are my pride and joy. I feel like if you make school interesting, the students will want to learn. On Friday, the students pick something during lunch that they want to do in order to feel good about themselves," Tiffaney explains.

In fact, on one Friday in Ms. Whyte's class, you could even find a group of sweet pre-teen girls gathered up for a manicure! This was an incentive for the girls in the class. They had parental permission for the manicure day and traded in tickets to earn this special reward during their lunch time. That level of extra special attention goes such a long way toward building an amazing school experience for kids that age! Tiffaney explains that "one way of increasing student engagement is finding out what they love to do. Now who doesn't love getting their nails polished by their favorite teachers?"

Ms. Whyte's care for students does not stop there. She recently traveled to Ghana for an incredible experience that refreshed her as a teacher, encouraged her to fight to do even better, and inspired the title of this article, and her motto, "Teach one, impact many." She shares a bit about the influence of this trip:

"I loved Ghana! It was a remarkable experience. Ghana is rich in resources. The people were humble and friendly. I learned that as educators, we are impacting the world, not just a classroom. I thought I was going to inspire teachers in another country, but what ended up happening is that they inspired and encouraged me!

These educators teach daily with sometimes over a hundred students with little supplies, or even without desks. Those educators inspired me to do better! Make an IMPACT daily! Stop COMPLAINING! Show up EXCITED every day! FIGHT harder for what my students need and want!

Most importantly, they INSPIRED me to FALL in love with EDUCATION all over again! Actually, my teeshirt design "Teach One, Impact Many" came from that experience."

Noticing that students would just lay down on the floor with their papers when they didn't have chairs, tables, or desks, Tiffaney observed, " You would think that education is not valued because of the extreme learning environment. However, students come from far away in order to be in the classroom. Some schools do not even supply students with a snack or lunch. Talk about discipline.

I remember going into one classroom and splitting a cracker numerous ways for all the students to eat something. In some classrooms, the students are sharing pencils just to get the work done.

When you walk into the classroom, all the students rise and greet you. It was pleasant to see all the smiling faces every day for two months.

One time, it rained heavily at my school. I got there, and not one teacher was there. There were over 200 or 300 students all in the classroom waiting for their teachers to arrive. I was like, "Oh my, none of the students are fighting!" The best part was, they didn't understand me, but didn't want me to leave. They followed my car down the highway.

At the end of my teaching experience, I was able to see most of Ghana in 3 days. It is a beautiful country. I am planning on going again very soon. I still keep in contact with my teacher friends there."

Back in Tiffaney's own classroom, she takes it one day at a time. Her advice is to " Do what you can - when you can!" To balance the challenges of being a mom and a teacher, while running a business, she says " I just do it! I am a single mother of two children. All my life I had to balance work, life and being a mom. I had my daughter as a young adult in college which forced me to be responsible and strong."

Like most teachers, she wants to give the kids her all, whenever she possibly can. One of the biggest challenges facing educators in her area is that special ed. teachers are just not remaining in the field. Tiffaney shares, "I teach because I love children. I am a Special Educator because I love when that lightbulb goes off in my students and they accomplish their goal. Becoming a teacher has always been a lifelong dream for me. I want my students to embrace all the highs in learning and absolutely always do their best. When learning is fun, it does not ever seem like hard work."

At the end of the day, even an teacher who is this dedicated needs a creative outlet. Tiffaney's goal with designing tees, vinyl designs, and stickers is to "empower educators to dress and be their best." She says, " I always love designing new outfits and creating fashion out of nothing. I am a creative soul. It has always been a hobby of mine."

photography by Kay Hillman
@MomentswithMKphotography

10 QUICK Q'S
with tiffaney

Give us a few fun tidbibts about yourself.
I love to eat (lol). I love having a good time (Life of the party and classroom). Laughing and smiling is contagious. I also love celebrating birthdays!

Tell us about starting your t-shirt business.
I actually got started by mistake. I knew I wanted to open a business. It was going to be creating a planner for teachers. I had the name, design, and concept. Months of preparation went into me getting ready to start designing the inside of the planner. However, I always loved graphic tees. One morning in April 2018, I woke up and switched from planner to tees. Instantly, I created my first design, not even giving it much thought: #Teach. One word; however, very powerful. From that day, I have been creating t-shirts.

What do most people not realize about creating t-shirts and stickers?
It takes a lot of creativity. I have a team of friends and family. I call them my A-Team (lol). They are the hardest critics. However, if it passes their rigorous questions that means it's a WINNER!

Share your favorite teacher hack or trick.
I love Post-Its. My students love it when I leave cute reminders typed out on a post-it. They think it's magic.

Share your favorite non-teaching hack or trick.
I use burgundy eye pencil as lipstick.

What fills your soul?
My family, happiness, and the joy of friendship. My love languages are gifts. Receiving and giving. I love giving gifts.

Tell us about a mentor or teacher of your own.
My co-teacher last year was really good with resources and deconstructed the standards. I learned many things from her. She respected the children and they respected her. She was a walking resource.

How does your environment impact you?
Honestly, I am an emotionally moody person, so my energy depends on my mood. If the environment is not great, my energy is really quiet. It's funny because when I'm not high strung everybody asks "are you okay?" They can see from my facial expression that my mood is off.

How do you get inspired for the next new project or design?
Inspiration for me comes from students, conversations and life experiences. I can tell you what I was thinking or doing when I created every shirt design.

Share your top 5 tips!
Teachers love free gifts!
If you pop microwave popcorn in a full room, someone will ask.
Red & blue make purple!
Be kind, always, to everyone. You may need that person in your life.
Don't judge a book by its cover!

10 THINGS TO DO WHILE MONITORING A TEST

Monitoring a test, whether it's your own assessment of students or a state-issued standardized test, can be tedious, trite, and tiresome! You have to be on alert and actively monitoring your students, which may make you feel like you can't actually get anything done in these times. However, this is actually an ideal time to think about and do certain things for which you don't always have the time.

Monitoring Your Own Test

Walk Around and Grade Notebooks

If you give notebook grades in your classroom, take this time to walk around with a pen and give a quick grade on each student's open notebook. Each one should only take a quick scan, which ensures you have enough attention to actively monitor the test-taking. Plus, it saves your back from lugging a heavy bag of notebooks home!

Sneak In Subtle Exercises

Just by simply walking around the room, you are getting your blood pumping. Why not take this time to add in a few discreet exercises? Stand behind your teacher desk or podium, and do little heel raises until your calves burn. Then, walk a lap or two around the room, and do another set. You can try strengthening your hamstrings by standing behind a chair and gently kicking one foot back so your heel hits the top of the thigh. Hold this for 5-10 seconds, then switch.

Get a Jump Start on Report Card Comments

Have you ever sat down at home to write your report card comments and struggled to recall details about a particular student? It's so much easier when they are sitting right in front of you in your familiar classroom! And when else do you have time to think about your students' behaviors while they're sitting quietly in front of you?

Tidy Up the Room

Monitor and clean simultaneously! Both are pretty mindless tasks, and yet, both need to be done. So, while walking around the testing students, pick up scraps of paper from the floor, pass back those papers that have been sitting on your desk and taking up space, and do anything else that allows you to move swiftly around the room, without distracting your students.

Check In With Each Student Individually

Start with any student who seems to be struggling or who you know has a more troublesome time with the subject. Even if your students seem to be working along just fine, get down to their level and whisper, "How's it going?" Their responses may surprise you, and eliminate some test anxiety.

Monitoring a State Issued Standardized Test

Actively monitoring during a standardized test requires strict attention on your students. Most guidelines are very specific. No sitting, no grading, no writing, no technology. When you have to actively monitor for days on end, it can be maddening. Here are some things to think about so you're planning ahead, getting deep thinking tasks done, and being mentally productive, instead of feeling bored out of your mind. This way, you won't feel like you're wasting your time.

Plan a Creative Brain Break

While walking around the room and keeping an eye on the testing, think over what the class will do on their next break. Whether it be 5, 10, or 15 minutes, those kids deserve a creative activity to give their brains a break! Maybe you can lead a game that involves movement, or split them into pairs and have them create a few words in a new language together. Think outside the box; you don't always have the luxury of time to think about these things!

Determine the Positive Attributes of Each Child

Although you can't write it down while monitoring a standardized test, considering positive characteristics of every student will definitely help you when it comes time to sit down with parents for a conference. Not to mention, it'll improve your mindset towards students who have more difficult tendencies. Teaching demands never leave enough time for sitting down to do this in one sitting. Now, you have plenty of time and your students sitting right in front of you. Look at each as you think about only that student.

Master the Week's Lesson Plans

You can't write down notes or draft out next week's plans while actively monitoring standardized testing, but you can read and review plans you have already made. Take this time to think about any prep involved and what else you can do to be fully prepared for upcoming lessons.

Contemplate Ways to Make your Room More Culturally Responsive

While walking by each desk, think about each student's background and culture. Do you know a lot about his or her background? Is this being represented in your classroom? Are there any activities you can do as a class to learn more about a holiday this culture celebrates? Do you have books representing this child's race or culture in your classroom library?

Evaluate Whether You Are Meeting Each Student's Needs

Now is the perfect time to look at each of your students, and ask yourself, "Am I doing everything in my power to help him or her learn?" Maybe you'll realize Kayla could use some one-on-one attention with fractions. Maybe you realize your extra shy student should be paired with a noticeably extroverted student the next time you divide up your class, to pull him out of his shell. Mull it over, and send good wishes or prayers as you watch each individual child.

BY KELLY BARENDT

VITAMINS & SUPPLEMENTS you didn't know could fit your needs

Do you crouch down to the level of a small child more than a few times a day? Are you exposed to a lot of germs? Are you on your feet all day? Do you spend a significant amount of time looking at your phone or laptop? Do you get sick often when the temperatures drop? Do you find yourself craving sunshine, especially during the winter when seeing the sun is rare? Do you ever feel so stressed out that it starts to affect your mood, your behaviors, and those around you?

As a teacher, you have specific health needs that correspond to the daily demands on your body. Chances are there is probably at least one area in which your health could improve. You may not have considered that there's probably a vitamin or supplement for the challenges you are facing. It may be time to address a problem or take preventive care. We've rounded up some common health problems that you probably did not realize can be improved by taking a vitamin or supplement! Always consult with your doctor before adding any supplement to your diet.

STRESS RELIEF

As a teacher, you work tirelessly day in and day out, constantly thinking about your students. Depending on your school, the problems will vary, but the one similarity between all teachers is that you are undeniably stressed, at least sometimes.

Magnesium can provide tons of benefits, including muscle tension relief, improved nutrient absorption, improved circulation, and stress relief. In fact, Magnesium is involved in over 300 chemical reactions in the body. You get a lot of Magnesium from food you regularly eat, like leafy greens and nuts, but many people still have low levels of Magnesium. Magnesium is best absorbed through the skin. The skin is the body's largest organ, and as such, has an amazing ability to absorb, filter toxins, and deliver nutrients to the body. Instead of taking an oral supplement, try soaking in a few cups (yes, *cups*) of Epsom Salts or Magnesium Flakes in a warm bath.

SEASONAL SUPPORT

Do you find yourself missing the sun in the winter? Seasonal Affective Disorder (SAD) is a common type of depression that usually affects individuals at the start of winter. The combination of cold weather and less sunshine can seriously affect people. Symptoms include having low energy, feeling depressed, losing interest in activities you once enjoyed, having difficulty sleeping, and experiencing changes in weight.

There are 4 major types of treatment for SAD, including medication, light therapy, psychotherapy, and Vitamin D3 supplementation. Although there are contradictory findings about the effectiveness of Vitamin D, it could be worth mentioning to your doctor if you believe you are experiencing SAD.

HEART HEALTH

Coenzyme Q10 could be an excellent supplement to add to your daily routine. CoQ10 is an antioxidant that the body naturally produces, but age and some diseases are linked to a deficiency of this chemical. CoQ10 has been found to provide heart benefits, help with energy, and protect cells, while deficiency has been linked to heart disease and cancer.

Kelly Barendt

IMMUNE SUPPORT

As a teacher, you absolutely need a strong immune system. It's simply non-negotiable when you have hundreds of teenagers cycling through your classroom and hallways, or you have small children's hands touching everything. There are only so many times you can say, "Remember to cough like a vampire!" (or into the crook of your elbow).

If you're like most teachers, you want to do everything in your power to prevent sickness and build up your immune system. The top three vitamins to boost your immune system are Vitamins C, B6, and E. However, experts say it's best to get these vitamins through food rather than supplements. The best way to do this is by eating a variety of colors of fruits and vegetables.

If you find yourself coming down with a common cold, you may want to look into taking zinc lozenges. According to the National Institute of Health's Fact Sheet, zinc lozenges may reduce the duration and severity of the common cold, especially if taken soon after the onset of illness.

EYE HEALTH

Age-related macular degeneration (AMD) and cataracts are some of the leading causes of vision impairment and blindness in the U.S., and clinical studies show that both increase significantly after age 60. So, the National Institute of Health enrolled more than 5,000 people with AMD in a study called AREDS. AREDS stands for Age-Related Eye Disease Study.

In 2001, researchers reported that high levels of antioxidants and zinc significantly reduce the risk of advanced AMD and its associated vision loss. They created the AREDS formulation, which contains vitamin C, vitamin E, beta-carotene, zinc and copper. Then, in 2006, this same research group developed AREDS2 with slight modifications.

Rates of AMD used to increase after age 65, but now increase after just 60. Experts wonder if this has to do with increased screen time in front of TVs, phones, laptops, tablets, etc. If you're someone who spends a lot of time in front of a screen, you might want to ask your doctor about AREDS or AREDS2, since the screen time is essentially aging your eyes faster.

JOINT STRENGTH

If you teach little ones, you're probably doing a lot of bending, crouching, kneeling, and just movement in general. Even with older students, you still do a lot of moving. As you age, you want your body to cooperate and perform these movements with ease. Whether you want to prevent joint pain or ease current problems, you should consider taking Boswellia.

Boswellia, or Indian Frankincense, is an herbal extract from a tree found in India, *Boswellia serrata*. It's been found that Boswellia can be a helpful anti-inflammatory and painkiller. It's been used to treat conditions like osteoarthritis and rheumatoid arthritis. It also promotes respiratory health. Ask your doctor about it if your joints are a concern.

HORMONE REGULATION

If you are a woman and suffer from PMS symptoms like cramps, headaches, bloating, irritability, and lethargy, you should ask your doctor about adding Borage to your list of daily vitamins. Borage oil, from the seeds of the *Borago officinalis* plant, has been found to help regulate women's hormones throughout their cycles.

Borage seed oil is one of the few plant sources of the essential fatty acid gamma-linolenic acid (GLA). Women with PMS are frequently deficient in GLA and have difficulty making more. Some studies show that supplementing with borage could help some women to bring up their levels of GLA and finally offer them relief from PMS symptoms.

Many vitamins can be found already in your diet, and taking a pill as a supplement could mean you are overdoing it and could be doing harm. Always consult with your doctor first. Vitamins and supplements do not have safety regulations or efficacy testing. Be sure to buy from a trusted source or you could be wasting your money.

Classroom Tour

THE TEACHER HOUSE

■■■■■■■■■■■■■■■■■■■■■■■■■■

Krista Luedtke
6th Grade
@theteacherhouse

Lately, classroom decor trends have covered a wide range of "themed" concepts, including llamas, owls, and even pineapples. Instead of jumping on board with all the latest hot design schemes, Krista, a 6th grade teacher in a rural area, has gone back to the basics.

The pure simplicity of her black and white room offers a beautiful, but soothing contrast. The two-toned classroom, with tiny sprinkles of color distributed here and there allows for a very calm environment. Krista shares, "My students love how 'clean' it is and the different seating options! We have high tables, low tables, desks, stools, comfy chairs, pillows, etc."

This 6th grade class is housed in a K-12 building in a small town. Krista explains, "I have a wide variety of learners in my classroom. I teach at the same school that I went to!

My first year of teaching, I taught kindergarten. Fast forward seven years later, and I am now teaching that same group of kids, but in 6th grade! It has been such a fun year.

This bulletin board (right) houses our classroom happenings! I bought this white board calendar from Hobby Lobby and used command strips to hang it up. I use it for important dates and birthdays. My kids reference this space often," says Mrs. Luedtke.

She explains that this handy setup notes any testing days and other events, and helps "keep my students AND me on track. I train my kiddos to use this instead of always asking me when things are.

This calendar is gold. It's dry erase and hung up so everyone can see it." What she loves most is, "I don't have to change anything out, just erase and start a new month! The only thing I change out are those motivational posters/quotes below the calendar."

Krista is graciously inviting us into her classroom for a tour, so flip through to see how she uses each area in her black and white room in the next few pages.

Setting and reaching goals is a life skill needed for success and happiness. Setting goals helps create responsibility for ourselves. I can set goals to help my brain grow.

Taking care of our body is important. Busy bodies need regular showering, brushing teeth, and clean clothes. I can keep my body clean.

It is in our human nature to want to be included. A sense of belonging improves motivation, health, and happiness. I can choose to invite and include everyone.

A Journal is a personal place to write down our thoughts, feelings or ideas. I can write in a journal to reflect, set goals, free write, & more.

Classroom HAPPENINGS

MONTH

SUNDAY	MONDAY	TUESDAY	WEDNESDAY	THURSDAY	FRIDAY	SATURDAY

TODAY'S CHALLENGE
COMPLIMENT A CLASSMATE.

Work hard and Be kind

Believe in you

Good vibes only

The unique alphabet focuses on a healthy body and healthy mind and portrays terms like "breathe," "create," "dream," and "kindness."

Try painting one wall in a dark color. You'll be surprised by how much it increases the cozy feeling, and if you have plenty of white, it won't make your space too dark at all!

The classroom has many different seating options. To make the low round table work for students who want to sit on the floor, the custodial staff cut the legs down to a lower height. Students can work at this table with pillows, or they can enjoy the other seating choices, which include regular desks and chairs, comfy upholstered chairs, or the tall table with stools.

Krista adds to the room slowly, often only incorporating one new key item each year. This helps keep the costs reasonable, and spread out over time. The students always come back to notice all the differences from the previous year!

She recommends trying to add small elements to the space each year, starting with items like rugs, fun chairs, lamps with softer lighting, motivational prints, pillows that add comfort, or alternate work station options like lap desks.

Where do you find the pieces you need for your classroom?

I find my items at various stores such as Target, Ikea, or Dollar Tree. I have also used DonorsChoose for some of the furniture in my room.

Share your favorite teacher hack.

Dry shampoo - the best thing since sliced bread!!! Major time saver!

What's the best teaching advice you've ever received?

That all kids want/need is to feel like they belong.

What do you want to tell the teachers of the world?

Keep being the best version of you! Kids need you!

To create the tall table, where students can perch on stools, Krista just placed inexpensive bed risers under the legs of a standard classroom table.

SNOWDAYMAGAZINE.COM | 37

"Our supply station, or "one stop shop" is the perfect place for all the things students need. My favorite spot is the lost and found. It's a great hack for finding random things in your classroom or for all of those pencils that seem to love the floor!" (left)

5 Tips for Engaging Students after a Long Break

>> Welcome students back with a personalized note in their locker/desk.

>> Change something in your classroom- the layout, seating arrangement, etc.

>> Start a novel study or group project.

>> Set up a new system for behavior - reward system, class challenge, etc.

>> Set goals and individually track their progress.

Students in Mrs. Luedtke's room sign contracts that include self-control, respect, and a promise to challenge themselves. After creating a list of hopes and dreams, they work together to establish rules. They keep a visual reminder of their goals up all year.

Since they work from the beginning to always be sure to respect their environment, Krista can allow students to come right into her teacher zone and join her at the horseshoe table. She claims it was the "best decision" to push her desk up against the wall. Even though the table is now her primary workspace, and the desk has become just storage, she still has kids join her at her work table, and its "so much easier!" They write directly on the table with whiteboard markers.

"My teacher area has been a work in progress throughout my seven years teaching, but I have finally figured out what works best for me and my students! I still have a desk for my computer and personal items, but then I have a big table that is right nearby. I am able to work with students at that table in a small group setting or one on one if need be. I have learned that my students love to sit at that table with me. The table also acts as a white board so it is perfect for teaching lessons!"

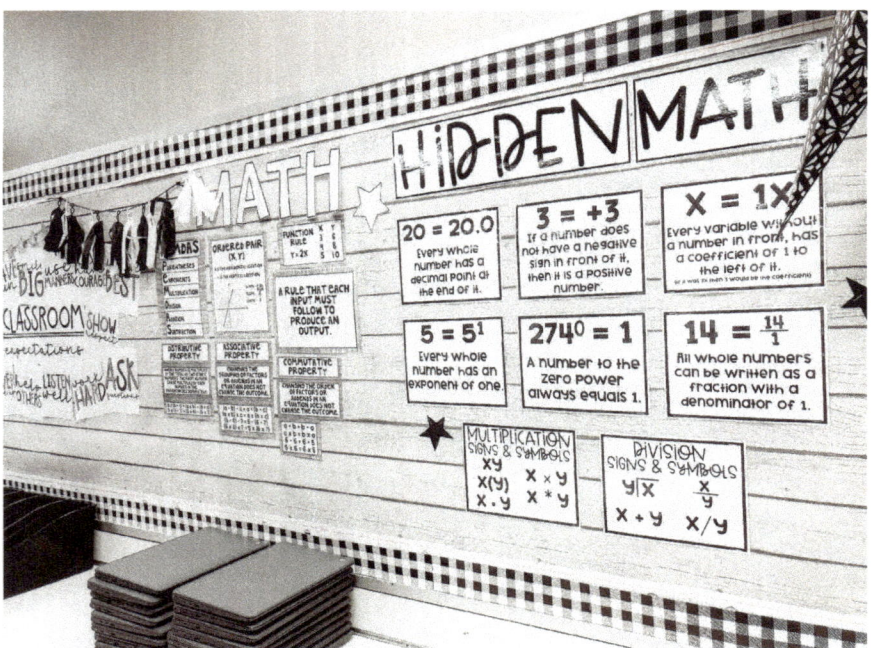

Krista has noticed that in math class, her students do best with whole-group lessons. She sometimes chooses this over stations or small group coaching, despite the fact that it may be "frowned upon" these days. She created these "hidden math" posters to support her students.

When it comes to bulletin boards, Krista recommends finding content that you can keep up all year, and she chooses the paper brand "better than paper" for bulletin board backdrops that need to be durable and stay up all year. It holds up well, even when you remove the staples, because of its vinyl-like texture. For the printed sheets, she sticks to her black and white theme, partly because the black ink is cheaper (and her only option when she prints at school), and partly because then "everything matches!"

"Our school has a very "small town" feel. I love being a part of that culture. I work to create a safe and positive environment in my classroom. I want my students to feel confident so that they can be their best selves. When a student feels this way, they are able to perform at a higher level - both academically and socially," Krista explains.

In addition to wanting her students to thrive in these ways, Krista also works to be her own "best self." She says, "If I prioritize nurturing my whole self, I find myself being a better teacher. In order to do that, I am sure to eat healthy during the week, exercise, sleep, and socialize. It is important to keep school at school! I have done a few DIY projects around my home and painted all of the walls in my house, my kitchen cabinets, trim, staircase, and a hutch. Now, with that labor of love complete, I enjoy filling the house with decor!

For more details about items in this classroom, a peek into Krista's home life, and teaching tips and inspiration, follow her @theteacherhouse on Instagram.

"Our math board is a place I find students walking over to look at often! Throughout the year we add more and more to the board as we go through our math lessons." (above)

"This wall is a view of our bulletin boards that we use to help us with our learning. We have a board for reading, writing, and theme. Theme is a very challenging concept in 6th grade and we use this board throughout the entire school year as a reference. Our reading board houses an anchor chart that we use for a visual to help us remember various comprehension strategies. Our writing board is a great reminder for using the writing process. All of these serve as guides for my students." (right)

A SENSE OF ownership

You've seen it happen. Parents team up to fundraise for months. Administrators work extra hours to make plans come together. Teachers spend every waking hour trying to do our best for our students. And then all the work and high hopes for the project, plan, or initiative feel wasted when certain groups of students respond negatively or fail to appreciate all the effort.

The lack of gratitude we sometimes see from children and teens can be so deflating. Why do they not realize how much we have sacrificed? How can they fail to understand and appreciate the hard work that so many people put forth just to give them this new playground, new classroom furnishing, or big event?

If you've seen students beating up lockers that their parents worked so hard raising funds to replace, or you notice them trashing the new seating options you spent your own money on, you may feel irritated and not know what the problem is. A sense of entitlement is probably at the root of it. To combat this, work to instill ownership.

When students are invested in the process of attaining and caring for their environment, their special events, and their materials, they'll be much more grateful, and as an added benefit, they will protect and maintain it all with much more care.

"Today was the opening day of this brand new middle school. We built it from the ground up. I was filled with pride this morning as I gazed down the long, spotless hallway lined with glossy, new lockers, as we waited for students to arrive. All the hard work, dedication, and money was about to pay off.

Fast forward to the end of the day, and my heart sank; our lovely new middle school was left in complete chaos and disarray. The hallways were a mess with papers, pencils, and trash. Multiple lockers were left open, and one was already jammed shut from being slammed too hard. The restrooms were a disaster; it seemed that no one placed their paper towel in the trash bin after drying their hands, a sink drain was clogged, and someone even wrote a joke in the bathroom stall. There were tiny bits of trash throughout the hallway, and pencils, paper scraps, and even gum wrappers scattered across all the classroom floors."

It is easy for some students to develop an attitude of entitlement, because they are so used to their circumstances. If you are noticing any of these symptoms of an entitled attitude, first take a day to show your students what they take for granted, then work to build in more opportunities for them to take ownership in their classroom and their education.

Exposing them to less fortunate students in different learning environments can help children or teens understand their affluent and fortunate circumstances are not to be taken for granted. For example, our students would be shocked to hear that students at Our Lady of Nazareth in Nairobi, Kenya generally do not have anything to eat at home. They live in the Mukuru slum (The name translates to "garbage dump") and go to school hungry, especially after the weekend. They are incredibly grateful for their education and the fact they they can get food at school, and hopefully a chance to move on to high school and escape poverty. In fact, they are so desperate to learn, that when a teacher walks out of the room, a student hops right up to continue at the board. They feel that every second of class time is precious. Education is the key to getting out of the slum. A very small percentage will ever go on to high school, and the ultimate dream is to get to go to college or get out of the area and be able to bring back enough money to help their families.

Show your class some online photos of students their own age in another country. Help them to feel gratitude for the fact that they can count on having a pair of shoes so they can go to school every day, instead of alternating with their siblings. Have a conversation with your students about the beautiful learning environment they have here, and their abundant opportunities.

To work toward lessening the problem of entitlement in their own situation, kids need to feel connected to the classroom and feel a sense of ownership. They are used to walking into a room and having it set up for them. This naturally makes them believe you and the school are responsible for cleaning and maintaining. When you shift your approach and allow the class to take on some of the accountability, they will gain a sense of ownership over the classroom. They can then slowly develop a sense of pride, and will no longer rip things, peel at their desk tags, or leave messes on the floor.

Start with meaningful jobs that create, enhance, and maintain the environment. Have frequent meaningful conversations to encourage gratitude for the details they never think about or take for granted.

It's important that students are exposed to other stories, and take ownership and responsibility for their education. They need to learn to practice gratitude for their blessings, as well as responsibility for their actions. These are important skills they will carry through life.

> "IT IS EASY, WHEN YOU ARE YOUNG, TO BELIEVE THAT WHAT YOU DESIRE IS NO LESS THAN WHAT YOU DESERVE, TO ASSUME THAT IF YOU WANT SOMETHING BADLY ENOUGH, IT IS YOUR GOD-GIVEN RIGHT TO HAVE IT." >> JON KRAKAUER

CULTIVATING & CREATING *ownership* TO CONQUER ENTITLEMENT

CUSTOMIZE MAILBOXES, LOCKERS, & DESKS

Many classrooms have designated mailboxes for each student, and you may be spending a significant amount of time before the start of the school year creating and attaching a label to each student's compartment, only to realize they're starting to peel off in a matter of a few weeks or months. The students just don't seem to reach into their mailbox with care. Try having your students create their own labels at the start of the school year. You can print sticker sheets with labels and have your class simply write their names, or try letting them get creative by writing their names in a fancy way. Whichever way you choose, students now have a sense of ownership over their mailbox, and will put in effort to keep it nice. If you have name tags on your desks or tables, you can implement this there, too.

DESIGN WALL DECOR

Let your students design the bulletin board or decide what should go on the wall. This encourages them to feel like the classroom is theirs; they will take pride in it. They have gotten used to you and previous teachers doing it all for them. You can take a class vote on ideas you provide or give your students more authority and room for creativity!

BUILD A CLASSROOM LIBRARY

If you have a classroom library, allow students to help you organize books into categories. Obviously, their age level determines how much responsibility to hand off, but even with little ones, you can guide conversations during the first week of school to determine which books should go together.

CREATE MORE MEANINGFUL CLASSROOM JOBS

To delegate ownership and responsibility, create meaningful classroom jobs. To create tasks and chores that will actually contribute, don't just think of typical ways that students can help; think of ways to make your classroom run more efficiently. Ask yourself: "What tasks am I currently doing that could be transferred to students' responsibility?"

Of course, classroom jobs are most popularly seen in elementary classrooms, but if you teach older kids, you can make slight adaptations and additions. To make classroom jobs more age-appropriate for secondary students, you can do things like implement job applications and hold interviews.

Don't be afraid to customize jobs to actual skills, rather than randomizing. A community is about each person contributing according to his/her talents and personal characteristics. It does not always have to look fair or equal.

Tech Team:
Whether your classroom uses chromebooks, tablets, or some other type of technological device, select a few students to manage the "technology station". Some kids have a natural knack for this. It will teach your class responsibility to keep devices charged and for younger students, it reinforces the importance of being safe and gentle with devices. Students with a true gift for tech troubleshooting can even become your school's own squad, helping teachers and other students with tech issues during study hall.

Jobs for Early Birds:
For students who arrive early on a daily basis, assign tasks that help jumpstart the day. Have student(s) write a message on the board, (that you scribbled on a post-it), then gradually grant more and more authority in creating the message. If your lesson requires specific materials or handouts, have them placed in a designated area, so a student knows to pass them out.

Classroom Secretary:
Delegate one student to be the classroom secretary, who manages work for absent students. They can record the day's tasks, collect handouts/materials, and make sure the absent student gets them.

Paper Managers:
Select one or two students to be responsible for collecting papers that need to be sent home. They can distribute the handouts into all of your students' mailboxes.

> *The creative process is a process of surrender, not control.* >> Julia Cameron

9 WAYS TO BUST OUT OF A Creative Rut

Tapping into creative brain waves decreases dementia, boosts CD4+ lymphocytes to keep you physically healthy, and reduces stress and anxiety.

When your mind and soul are not being used to produce and create, you start to suffer as a human. Being crafty, trying new things, and putting something forth into the world leads to health benefits.

Boost your brain function and your mental health by getting creative! Your physical body will flourish as well, since creative brain activity has been linked to a stronger immune system. Let your cognitive function start to spike, and get happy with a dopamine rush by unblocking your creative flow!

Getting out of a creative rut can mean spicing up your date night, trying a new outfit combo, tackling a home project, or even just incorporating a new recipe into your dinner plan this week. Here are some ways to help unlock your own creative brainwaves.

what to do when you're not feeling inspired

Repurposing
Upcycle something you already own. Transforming an item to give it new life is a great halfway project, since it requires less ingenuity than creating something completely new from scratch. This will help you ease in slowly and tap into the creative vibes that are hiding underneath the surface of your mind.

Comedy
Researchers from the University of Maryland found that watching something funny can double the brain's capacity for mental flexibility. Engage your brain by taking a stand-up comedy class, or watching a few minutes of a comedy show.

Input Before Output
Browse, seek, and get inspired. Your brain may be overflowing such that you cannot find the source of any original vision, or it may be empty and need some input before it's ready to produce. Listen to a podcast, read a book, scroll through Pinterest, or flip through a magazine that appeals to you. Before long, you'll likely switch from the mode of soaking it up over into an inventive "output" state.

Rest
Take a nap. Your brain will work while you sleep. Or, in a longer phase of disinterest, try disconnecting to give yourself a break for a whole season. Both immediate sleep as well as long cycles of freshness and off-times reflect the natural ups and downs of creative flow.

Change a Routine
Switch it up to invite new thoughts and ideas. Imagination is fueled when you get out of the ordinary. Spice up your morning routine, or try doing something completely different on your lunch break or before bed. Make space for the new and novel in your life.

Exercise
A half hour of exercise offers a creative boost that lasts for hours. Go out for a walk or jog, and before long, the empty space in your mind (or the distracting thoughts) will flow into a new state of imagination.

Shifting the Focal Point
If you've got a case of writer's block, turn your chair to face the window. Or try a more drastic change of scenery by getting out of the house or classroom. Set up your workstation at a coffee shop or your local library. Try taking your project out to a park. You can even try changing up the format completely. Instead of writing your ideas, try dictating them aloud into a phone app. When the output comes in a different form, you may be surprised at the way the flow of your thoughts, words, and ideas can change too!

Binaural Beats
A neuroscience study published on NCBI found that some individuals show an increase in divergent thinking when listening to special binaural beats in different frequencies. You can find tracks to listen to online if you'd like to give it a try.

Fuel Up
What you consume will impact your brain's abilities. Fuel your gut for creativity by eating plenty of antioxidants, like blueberries, particularly in the morning. The serotonin levels in the brain usually peak in the morning as well, priming your brain for creativity. Start your day with plenty of protein to keep those creative juices flowing.

> *When you've exhausted all the possibilities, remember this: you haven't.* >> Thomas Edison

TEN MINUTE TEST-RUN PROJECTS TO SEE WHAT LIGHTS YOU UP

Grab a pair of "blank" dangly earring hooks from the craft store. Add a feather, pom pom, metallic bead, or other accent to design your own pair of earrings that fit your style.

Color a page of an adult coloring book using copic markers. They are so satisfying to use! Frame it if you love your work.

Collect a handful of your favorite family photos and make a photo collage. Find one unique way to make it special, either in the way you arrange it, or the materials you use to display it.

Redecorate a room in your home by "shopping" the rest of your house. Clear all decor items from the room, rearrange the furniture, and then walk around the rest of your home, gathering items or accent furniture pieces from other rooms to move. It will feel fresh, and give you opportunities to think about the items you already own in different ways.

Make a scavenger hunt for your students. Try something content-based, or just make it a fun reward. They can earn new clues all day long.

Plan a new dinner recipe by selecting two completely different recipes that you've never tried before, and taking elements of each to develop a new meal idea that combines them both.

Other Sources: Forbes, Medical News Today

TEACHING GRATITUDE

by Shannon Gareau

"If the only prayer you said in your whole life was, 'thank you,' that would suffice." >> Meister Eckhart

BATTLING ENTITLEMENT

"I can't wait to see the looks on their faces! They will be so excited," I thought to myself as I set up the room for our class Christmas party. I had stayed late after school to transform our classroom into a winter wonderland and set up the room with games, crafts and fun. The next day, my 5th graders came into the room and the festivities began! All of my well thought out plans and detail-oriented activities were running smoothly, and the morning flew by. As the kids shuffled out to recess and lunch, I asked some of my students how they enjoyed the morning. "It was alright, but I'm most excited for recess," said one of the kids. "It was fun, but I would rather have just watched a movie," said another. "Mr. Smith's class got donuts for their morning party" said another. My heart sank. I had put so much time and effort into making the morning fun, and it was met with ingratitude and lack of appreciation.

Students today show signs of entitlement more than ever before. This is partly because many students are accustomed to being rewarded for simply participating. They often learn less because they don't feel the need to do the work. So how do we, as teachers, combat this entitled attitude in the classroom? The answer lies in teaching our students the importance and benefits of gratitude, and encouraging them to practice gratitude in their daily lives.

The benefits of putting an emphasis on gratitude in your classroom (and in your own personal life) are tremendous! Not only does gratitude help prevent an entitled attitude, but gratitude improves classroom culture, and helps to ensure happiness and success in our students. Teaching your students gratitude is sure to affect everyone in a positive way!

Ensure Happiness and Success

Feeling grateful can positively affect your mental, emotional, and physical health, and ultimately help you achieve the life you want. According to an article by Geoffrey James, "People who approach life with a sense of gratitude are constantly aware of what's wonderful in their life. Because they enjoy the fruits of their successes, they seek out more success. And when things don't go as planned, people who are grateful can put failure into perspective." Isn't that what we, as teachers, ultimately want for our students? We want them to seek out success and learn from their mistakes. Encouraging and teaching gratitude will help them develop these important life skills, and help them achieve their best.

Teaching Gratitude

So where do we begin teaching classroom gratitude? How do we help our students not only understand the benefits of gratitude, but help them to feel deep gratitude and practice it in their own lives? Here are a few ideas of ways to plant the seeds of gratitude and foster an attitude of gratitude in your classroom.

CLASSROOM STRATEGIES >>>>>>>>>>>>>>>>>>>>>>>>>>>>>>>>>>>>

Gratitude Journal

An effective way to teach gratitude in your classroom is by introducing gratitude journals. Students can carry composition notebooks, or keep an online portfolio, and each day, write three specific things they are thankful for. The key is to be as specific as possible. So instead of writing, "I'm thankful for breakfast," encourage them to write "I'm thankful for the bowl of cereal and the banana I ate this morning." Gratitude journals only take a couple of minutes, but are immensely powerful in teaching gratitude.

In an article published by the *Greater Good Science Center at UC Berkeley*, the benefits of keeping a gratitude journal were discussed. This journaling practice helped promote a more grateful attitude among students. The article states, "For example, studies have found that more grateful adolescents are more interested and satisfied with their school lives, are more kind and helpful, and are more socially integrated. A few studies have found that gratitude journaling in the classroom can improve students' mood and that a curriculum designed to help students appreciate the benefits they have gained from others can successfully teach children to think more gratefully and to exhibit more grateful behavior."

Be a Role Model / Grateful Example

When I think about how I learned to be grateful, and show my appreciation towards others, I realize that it came from watching my parents. We all learn through examples and by watching others. Our students are watching us, to see if we practice what we preach and teach. In my own classroom, I make sure to point out things I am thankful for, no matter how small they may be.

Practicing gratitude yourself, and being open about it to your students, is the perfect way to help your students learn to practice gratitude as well. You can make sure you say thank you, show optimism, or even share anecdotes of how you are practicing gratitude.

I have also discovered that saying "thank you" to my students, for being helpful or doing something well, motivates them to work harder and say "thank you" to their fellow classmates. Expressing my gratitude for them is a very powerful tool in promoting a grateful spirit.

Showing Appreciation

Students often overlook those who provide service for them, at school and at home. Ask your students to write thank you cards for people who make their lives easier in ways they never even think about.

Start with a quick chat about the way the custodian ensures that there are enough desks for each child in each room, keeps the floor clean, and keeps the windows and HVAC system working properly so they can be comfortable all day. Help them take a moment to reflect on all the little things they take for granted. You can even make a list on the board by having students contribute ideas of what the school nurse, custodian, secretary, librarian, etc. do for them each day behind the scenes.

Then, they can jot a note featuring one of these things that they are grateful for. This is worth taking time to do! Students who take a moment to think these things through will walk around forever with a different perspective of the people around them.

When teaching them, focus on empathy. Model putting yourself in someone else's shoes. Try sharing something with your students like "I am so grateful for Mr. Tim myself, because some days, there is such a mess on the floor in here and he has to stay late when I am heading home for dinner with my family. I wonder if we can do a better job keeping this room clean so that he can count on us for a quick sweep, and get home a few minutes earlier every night. I bet he'd really appreciate that."

Gratitude Jar

The gratitude jar is something I recently started in my classroom that has been a very positive experience for my students and myself. In my classroom, I have a large jar with post-it notes sitting next to it. I encourage the students to write down little notes of gratitude throughout the week. I also challenge them to write about different experiences, classmates, family members, or staff each time they write a note of gratitude. On Fridays, I read the notes of gratitude out loud for the class. The students have the option of writing who the note is from, or they can remain anonymous. Both the students and I look forward to ending our week reading and sharing our notes of gratitude with each other. I have found that creating regular opportunities to share what they are grateful for really helps students focus on their blessings and positive experiences throughout the week.

Consistency is Key, but Variety Adds the Spice

Students love routine and consistency, so adding one of these ideas to the daily routine can help make practicing gratitude a habit. For example, starting the day with a few minutes of silent reflection and writing down three things they are thankful for in their gratitude journal can help the students learn to focus on their blessings, not their problems. This can help them start the day on a positive note and get them in the right mindset for the day ahead.

The downside to tying gratitude into something you routinely do is that it can start to lose its meaning. An article by Sumitha Bhandarkar, discusses the problem of this gratitude focus becoming a "rote routine" for kids, and how it's important to teach them to "be present" when practicing gratitude. In regard to gratitude feeling tedious, she explains that, " Such days will occur – that's OK. But as much as possible, make a concerted effort to actually be present and feel the gratitude." Having your students silently reflect, putting on peaceful music, and maybe even closing their eyes may help them feel and think deeply about the things they are grateful for.

Another way to make practicing gratitude a habit, without losing the meaning behind it, is to vary the different

"If you want to turn your life around, try thankfulness. It will change your life mightily."
>> Gerald Good

methods students use to focus on gratitude each month. For example, in my classroom, we usually spend the first few minutes of the day writing in our gratitude journals, but then I will give the students a different way to focus or "display" the things they are grateful for. In September, the students focused on things they were thankful for in nature and were able to choose a few to display on a picture of a tree that was hanging in my room. For the month of October, I asked the students to focus on things they were thankful for at school and we displayed them by writing them on a pumpkin in the classroom.

Each month, I try to change the focus and add a unique way to display their blessings. I've found that having a visual reminder about gratitude is also very helpful in developing an attitude of gratitude. Eventually, I will have the students choose the focus and a way to display them. I've found that giving them creativity and ownership over something that we routinely do helps keep it fresh and exciting for them.

Show your Students the Struggles and Sacrifices of Others

A powerful way to encourage gratitude in your classroom is to teach about students in less fortunate countries or situations. Our students are so used to being in their own bubble. Exposing them to these ideas really helps them see how grateful they should be. Even pulling up some web images of schools in other countries may help. Invite speakers to share their stories with the class. Talk to your students about the beautiful learning environment and opportunities they have.

This may also encourage your class to take it a step further and take on a class service project. In an article titled "Gratitude- The Antidote for Entitlement," Andy Smithson states, "Whether it is helping to make a meal for a sick neighbor, working in grandma's garden, or visiting a homebound widow, it is important to include our children in acts of service. When we allow them opportunities to forget themselves and recognize the greater needs of others, it can fill both us and them with gratitude for what we have." Serving others helps us experience and share genuine gratitude and love.

Explicitly Teach Social and Emotional Learning

Over the past two years, I have been spending time explicitly teaching my students social and emotional learning concepts, and have seen numerous benefits as a result. The students (and myself) have less anxiety, better focus, and an overall better attitude towards learning. Honestly, I wish I would have been taught these things as a kid!

In the classroom, we spend time discussing growth mindset, perseverance, empathy, gratitude, and mindfulness. Teaching mindfulness really helps the students focus on the present moment and helps them truly feel the gratitude they are expressing. Two resources I use to teach these concepts to my students are *ClassDojo.com* and *Calm.com*. These websites have a lot of great resources designed specifically for teachers to help teach these social and emotional concepts to your students.

4 WAYS TO CULTIVATE GRATITUDE IN YOURSELF

1) Gratitude Session
Start your day with a few minutes of intentionally focusing on whatever you're grateful for. Practice mindfulness, and do nothing else during that time, except focusing on the present and using your senses. In a post written by Leo Babauta entitled "Why Living a Life of Gratitude Can Make You Happy", he suggests "Take 2-3 minutes each morning to give thanks, to whoever or whatever you're grateful for. You don't have to do anything, other than close your eyes and silently give thanks. This one act can make a huge difference." Starting your morning this way can really help set the tone for a positive day!

2) Ask Yourself "What is going well?"
When things aren't going as planned, it is easy to focus on the negative and all that is going wrong. When things start to spiral out of control, it's hard to focus on the positive. Dr. Allison of *Simplified Psychology* suggests that asking yourself the question "What is going well today?" will help pull you out of that downward negative spiral. She says, "You are going to have to use every single ounce of energy to direct your brain to see the good. It won't want to. It will want to dwell on the negative, snowballing a few tough things into a full blown awful, terrible day. But you can choose to see the good." Asking yourself this one simple question can have a profound impact.

3) Visual Reminders
Having visual reminders around is a great way to help cultivate an attitude of gratitude. A post on *PsyBlog* suggests this tip by Dr. Robert Emmons explaining, "Two big obstacles to being grateful are simply forgetting and failing to be mindful. So leave a note of some kind reminding you to be grateful. It could be a post-it, an object in your home or another person to nudge you occasionally." Having a visual cue will help to remind you to practice gratitude on a more regular basis.

4) Try a Gratitude App
If keeping a paper journal doesn't appeal to you, try a gratitude app! There are a ton of great apps out there that can help make practicing gratitude a daily habit. We are attached to our phones, and it helps to have these automatic gratitude tools at our fingertips. *Gratitude* and *Happyfeed* are two apps that can help you transform your gratitude practice. They both will give you prompts to start a gratitude journal, daily reminders, tips, and inspirational quotes to make your gratitude journey more of a daily routine, and eventually a lifelong practice.

Psychologist Jeremy Dean, PhD, the founder and author of PsyBlog, conducted a gratitude experiment and found that practicing gratitude can increase happiness by

25%

Additional Sources: berkeley.edu, time.com, spring.org, Zen Habits, Psychology Today

> "Gratitude and attitude are not challenges; they are choices."
> >> Robert Braathe

SCIENTIFICALLY PROVEN BENEFITS OF GRATITUDE

Practicing gratitude affects all areas of life. Here are some surprising benefits of practicing gratitude:

Emotional
Emotional benefits of gratitude include a more calm and overall positive outlook on life. Gratitude reduces social comparisons and makes us less envious of others. It helps us to appreciate the accomplishments of friends and family, rather than feel jealous. A grateful attitude helps increase empathy and reduce aggression towards others.

Social
The social benefits of practicing gratitude include improved relationships with others. Those with a grateful attitude have deeper and healthier relationships. This happens because gratitude helps you acknowledge other people's contributions, which leads to better overall relationships.

Physical
According to a 2012 study published in *Personality and Individual Differences*, "Grateful people experience fewer aches and pains and report feeling healthier than other people." Individuals that practice gratitude have improved sleep, increased energy, are more likely to take care of their health, and exercise more frequently.

Career
Practicing gratitude has been shown to help improve decision making. These stronger decisions lead to increased productivity and more frequent goal achievement. These qualities will make you a valuable employee and help you achieve success in your career.

Temperament
People who approach life with a sense of gratitude have an overall improved self-esteem, are less self-centered, are less materialistic, and bounce back more easily when they face difficulties. Being grateful fosters resilience, and helps people put failure into perspective. A grateful attitude helps people appreciate all facets of life, and learn from challenges and mistakes

PASSING NOTES

> Gratitude is not only the greatest of virtues, but the parent of all the others.
> \>\> Marcus Tullius Cicero

What signs or symptoms help you recognize a need to enhance gratitude practices and habits?

When students become **unusually quiet or moody,** this suggests they may need help focusing on the positives. They probably have a legitimate reason to be sad. That is why gratitude tasks should be presented not as a judgement on the validity of their feelings, but a tool that they can use to **broaden their perspective to cope with and process their feelings.** Personally, I know I need this perspective boost when I am becoming stressed and bogged down in the details.

>> *Frances, Year 7-10*

I recognize a lack of gratitude when kids are only **focused on what is wrong** and not focused on what is good. We do a lot of mindfulness in my classroom and that includes gratitude work.

>> *LaRissa, high school*

I can identify a need for gratitude when a student expresses **frustration at a parent's (or teacher's) attempt to provide structure through setting behavior expectations.** Providing this type of structure for students is one of the most loving things we can do, both as parents and as educators.

>> *Angie, 7th grade ELA*

I can spot a need for gratitude when kids are acting spoiled or entitled. And for myself, it tends to pop up as feeling jealous of someone else, or sometimes as a **"why me" persecuted feeling.** I've finally started to recognize that envious or whiny voice in my head more quickly for what it is - a sign of disconnect with the gratitude I know I should be feeling. Redirecting that feeling into awareness that the grass is not always greener for someone else when you look deeper under the surface helps me to go back to spotting my own blessings and shift into feeling more abundance in my own life.

>> *Brigid, Editor*

What a great question! I'd say... Whenever I catch myself **grumbling or complaining,** it's almost always a sign that I have lost sight of the bigger picture and need to stop and count my blessings. There are so many wonderful things right in front of me!

>> *Aubrey, MS Math*

indicators of deception

HOW TO DETERMINE WHEN A STUDENT MAY BE LYING
USING 6 KEY SIGNALS THAT PRO INTERVIEWERS DEPEND ON

There are a handful of times each year as a teacher that you may find yourself in a tricky situation where you suspect a student may not be telling you the truth, but you just don't feel sure enough to know what your next steps should be. In some cases, your goal is not even necessarily to catch a student in the wrong, but for his/her own safety, you need to get an honest answer. Whether you suspect a child or teen of cheating on a test, stealing from a friend, or even hiding abuse, you often can only help by getting to the root of the problem.

To help uncover the truth, start watching for these six signals, labeled as "indicators of deception" by law enforcement professionals. A lot of people think that body language is the best way to catch a fib, but there can be many reasons for a change in body language. A stronger way to indicate an untruth is through careful listening to the words and phrases. Noticing two of these key signals within a five second period after asking the question will at least clue you in that the student may be hiding something, or is uncomfortable.

1 attacking the questioner

When asked a question, a person who is being deceptive may yell, go after the questioner, and sometimes even swear. If a student gets disproportionately upset, or says things like "How dare you ask me..." or "Who do you think you are? What gives you the right to accuse me?" be on alert for a fib. Another example is "My dad is a lawyer." or similar threats.

2 referral statements

An individual who is disguising the truth is likely to refer to previous statements when a question is rephrased or a topic comes up again. Watch for phrases like "just like I said before," or "I already told you..." If a student is telling the truth, they will be more likely to give a clear "no" answer and be willing to get straight to it without these referrals.

3 qualifying statements

Be on the lookout for words that leave wiggle room, like "usually," "basically," "sometimes," or "probably." Lying is psychologically difficult to do, and phrases including these words help someone to convice himself/herself that the statement is not a complete lie. It leaves room for being only halfway honest.

4 not answering the question

Talking in a circle around the question is a way to avoid answering it directly. Kids and teens can be surprisingly good at this. For example, if you ask a student why he/she has the same answers as a friend on a quiz, this would sound like "We're in the same class... It's just possible... Why would you think..." instead of coming right out and saying "We did not cheat."

5 convincing statement

An unrelated claim that features the child or teen's (or suspected abuser's) best qualities can sometimes be an attempt to redirect your attention. Be suspicious if a student points out ways that you should blindly trust and never doubt. This may sound like "I'm a straight A student," or "I've never been accused of anything! Don't you know I'm in the honors society?"

6 disproportionate punishment wish

Try asking the student what he/she thinks that the appropriate punishment for the particular offense should be. If the response is suspiciously lenient, you may want to follow up with more questions and keep watching for these signals. A student who is not hiding anything would feel that the logical and usual consequence would be warranted.

Once you do spot one of the above signs, your goal can now shift toward resolution. This is your clue that your gut feeling may have been right, and there is likely a lie or a half-truth coming out. At this point, stop the student from talking and take over. Lead the conversation toward an admission, making it clear that everything will be ok, and that you are here to teach, support, and resolve whatever the problem is. Help the student to relax, open up and get honest. Consequences will still be given, but show compassion as you guide the child through the next steps.

These clues are just meant to be signals to guide your decision-making. They are not foolproof, and serious matters may need additional professional intervention or support, but having this mental checklist may help you to continue training your own intuition. If you can sometimes spot a lie in more obvious cases, looking for these indicators will help you practice detecting it in trickier situations, always with the goal of helping our students stay safe, become better people, and get the support that they need.

Pro Tip:
It's easy to lie when asked a yes/no question. Keep questions open ended, and deceptive students are more likely to talk themselves into trouble. Never call a student a liar.

Much of the theory behind these now widely used techniques is the work of former CIA officers Philip Houston, Michael Floyd, and Susan Carnicero, who coauthored *Spy the Lie*, a book you can use to look further into this methodology.

"My goal is to promote clay as a healthy, therapeutic solution for people who may be suffering from anxiety, depression, or other mental illnesses."

MENTAL GROUNDING THROUGH

clay

BY SOPHIA GOLOVANEVSKAYA
@HOUND.CERAMICS
HOUNDCERAMICS.COM

I think most people don't realise just how much of a spiritual process ceramics actually is. The ceramicist starts off with a ball of mud which they transform into a vessel.

The clay is shaped, trimmed and carved. It goes through different stages of drying (all which are dependent on the weather) before its kiln firings.

The ceramicist must learn to let go of each piece before the firing process begins. Even the most experienced ceramicist remains at mercy of the kiln fire. When the final firing is over, our pieces emerge transformed and permanent.

I just got goosebumps writing that. I'm such a nerd.

Getting started - a stress remedy
I started ceramics as a personal pursuit for art therapy. My stress levels were out of control and I was really struggling with processing my emotions, as well as handling everyday tasks and responsibilities. I'm really lucky in that I've always known that I'm a creative person, so when things got hard, I knew I had to find a new creative outlet. Other people aren't that lucky; a lot of us don't even know what we like to do or what calms us down because we're so focused on corporate, financial, or family goals.

Working with clay grounded me and allowed me to process intense feelings of anxiety and depression. Now, I teach casual pottery workshops where people can come 'test-drive' a hobby and be a part of a safe, supportive, non-committal community for the day. Although clay can't cure mental illnesses, my goal is to promote clay as a healthy, therapeutic solution for people who may be suffering from anxiety, depression, or other mental illnesses.

A peek into the magic of ceramics
I love functional ceramics! The functionality of ceramics is definitely what attracted me to it in

SOPHIA
>> TEACHER
>> CERAMICS ARTIST
>> BUSINESS OWNER

the first place. Especially mugs. Making a mug is such a long, beautiful, and technical process.

There's something very sacred to me about making a mug and then using it to make myself a hot tea when I'm feeling anxious. That's very grounding for me. Anything functional that can be used to sustain our lives and bodies is my calling. Everything tastes much better in a handmade vessel!

I teach all ages. With kids from 6-12 y/o we usually make lots of animal sculptures together. I always allow the kids to explore their own creativity. The theme for the day might be frogs, but if you want to make a dragon, that's fine with me too! I really just want to see them interact with the clay. They always get so creative!

With adults and teenagers, our focus is usually functional ceramics such as mugs, bowls and vases. It's always so exciting to see how much intention and care people pour into their pieces.

I like to think that as well as ceramics, I also teach how to remain present in the moment. Clay demands your full attention 100% of the time. One of the most common pieces of positive feedback I get is that people who participate in my pottery workshops don't give any thought to what's stressing them out in their personal lives while working with clay. That's my ultimate goal!

Fill your space with things you love and that have meaning to you. The vibes will always be good!

Creative Roots

I was born in Australia to Ukrainian parents. I grew up speaking two languages, and still get them mixed up sometimes.

I love gardening. My favourite animal is a chicken. I studied a double degree at Curtin University in Anthropology/Sociology and Creative Writing.

I used to write poetry and even got some poems published in a couple of magazines! I hope that I'll eventually be able to combine my love for social work/youth work and ceramics for good.

Carving out Time to Create

For me it's just part of my routine. I need to make time to create just like I need to make time to clean, cook and pay my bills on time. If I don't, my mental health will take a dramatic turn for the worse.

Even if I don't have clay around me, I still need to do something. When I'm travelling I draw quite a bit, although I'm rubbish at it.

Create where/when you can. Dedicate one night of the week, or month, to do what you love. Don't think of creativity as just making art. Wear some silly/

cool clothes, collect dried leaves or flowers, cook an extra wholesome meal! Keep a journal where you can jot down your creative ideas, even if you can't act on them straight away. Look for creativity everywhere.

The Home Studio
Well, it's a bit of a dungeon at the moment. My office is my dining room table and my studio is my shed. It's small but I'm still so incredibly grateful for my own space. I get a lot of glazing done at my local public studio as well.

My environment can definitely impact me for better or worse. Ideally my space needs to be uncluttered for me to get lots of work done, but that's not always the case. As long as I have something beautiful to look at, like plants or some art from other local creatives, I'm content and can get stuff done. Fill your space with things you love and that have meaning to you. The vibes will always be good!

Inspiration for Teachers
My first pottery teacher is one of the funniest, most talented women I have ever met. It's like there's nothing she can't do. She has raised 4 renowned artists and can pretty much do any creative thing under the sun. I sincerely hope I have her level of energy and wit when I'm 75+! She's currently teaching my mum watercolour botanical painting.

Always encourage an interest in something, no matter how irrelevant it may be to the subject you're teaching. If more people felt encouraged we would have so much less stress and sadness in the world. Try and make connections between unlikely interests. Also, relate all your teachings back to nature and Earth. That is our number one calling.

Work & Style Transitions Over Time
It hasn't stopped! I'm a very indecisive person and I start to feel creatively blocked if I stick to one style for too long. That can be both good and bad. I'm always pushing myself to try new things, but I'm usually moving onto the next thing too quickly. It's a work in progress!

TELL US YOUR FAVORITE HACK.
Black tea and early grey tea brewed together with a little bit of soy milk. So yum!! And so much better than coffee.

WHAT ARE YOU MOST GRATEFUL FOR?
My parents for raising me and for always supporting my creativity and my ideas, no matter how dumb they may be sometimes. My partner for always making me believe I know what I'm doing, even through my manic stress episodes. And my dear friend Amber, for being my soul and support rolled up in a magic ball. And of course, I'm forever grateful for clay for always kicking me in the butt.

"Look for creativity everywhere."

Q & A with Sophia

HOW DO YOU BALANCE WORK AND LIFE?
...Ask me again in 3 years. It's a work in progress.

WHAT IS YOUR FAVORITE BOOK RIGHT NOW?
I recently read *We Need to Talk About Kevin* by Lionel Shriver and MAN that was a wild ride!

HOW DO YOU GET INSPIRED?
Reading, gardening, listening to music, looking at a variety of different types of art works and crafts. My number one form of inspiration for colour and form will always be nature.

WHAT DO YOU LISTEN TO?
I probably have the most eclectic taste in music compared to most people. I can get down to pretty much everything. When I'm creating though, I like to listen to more chill tunes like the blues. Anything with smooth or raw vocals. Alt-j, Winston Surfshirt and Rainbow Kitten Surprise are great modern examples.

WHAT FILLS YOUR SOUL?
Anything that makes me feel connected to the Earth.

The Real Truth About Teaching with Depression

Depression. Anxiety. Panic Attacks. PTSD. What do you think of when you hear those words? Do you imagine a terrified and lost individual crumpled in a corner? Do you think suicide, medications, hospitals, and therapy? Well I'm here to tell you that more and more, it's becoming the face of our teachers. Teaching with depression and anxiety is a very real thing and something I've lived with for over twenty years.

In 2017, it was found in an *American Federation of Teachers'* Educator Quality of Work Life Survey that 61% of teachers found their job "often" or "always" stressful. In addition, 58% of those surveyed also cited poor mental health as one of the reasons for their stress. Teaching is difficult. Studies say that the stress level and decision making required in teaching is comparable to brain surgeons and air traffic controllers, yet teachers are often degraded in society, and some people have even been known to say, "Those who can't, teach." When society has so little respect for the profession that spends more hours awake with the children of today than their own parents do, how is workplace depression even a surprise?

I not only have depression; I have major depressive disorder and bi-polar 2. This means I have intense bouts of massive chronic depression, but the high waves of feeling good never hit mania. I just cycle between exceedingly low and okay, all the time. Even when I'm having a great day, I don't feel ecstatic, gleeful, or get those endorphin highs; I rarely get past just feeling good, and it leads to many issues of miscommunication with others. What friends, family, students, and parents may perceive as irritation or a lack of warmth, is just my bi-polar rearing its head. I actually love teaching, enjoy my students very much, and love hugs, but I have trouble conveying that through body and facial language.

BY BRITTANY NAUJOK
OF "THE COLORADO CLASSROOM"
@COLORADO_CLASSROOM

A CANDID CONVERSATION AND
A SET OF **COPING STRATEGIES**

If that wasn't enough, I also suffer from anxiety, a heightened sense of hyper-vigilance, and an intense worry about anything and everything around me. When I lack the big picture or feel insecure or out of control, I question and question and question until I'm paralyzed with fear, and end up driving my loved ones insane with my worry, doubt, and intense questioning. It keeps me up at night and wakes me at two in the morning with random thoughts of failure and despair.

Lastly, there is PTSD, and I hate to even bring this one up because I feel like I do the men and women who serve our country and truly face the horrors of war an injustice when I say I have PTSD, but in some small way, I have my own form of this horrible disorder. Mine came after several years of being intensely bullied, badgered, and beaten down by administrators who wanted to see me gone. They made my life a living hell and made me feel like I was a failure time and time again. Anyone who spoke up on my behalf was quickly and permanently dismissed, or horribly badgered themselves.

Even my contribution to education and my eleven years of service was erased in just under two years. It was horrible and made me hate myself even more intensely than I thought possible. Today, this disorder causes me to be paranoid of others' intent, skittish, and scared. I often loathe myself and my decisions, blaming myself for anything and everything that happens, because that's what I was told repeatedly for years on end. It plays with my sense of reality and challenges my belief in myself on an almost daily basis.

These three disorders have combined to make for one interesting individual. My husband of 27 years is a saint for putting up with me and all my mood swings, bouts of depression, and feelings of worthlessness. I did my best to hide it from my kids for many years, but they also have put up with a lot and have dealt with a mom who is not always at her best.

Despite all of that, I love hugs and to be cuddled, despite having resting "B*" face. Time in the mountains, exploring the hills and streams gives my soul joy. I cherish the moments when I get to see a student light up with revelation, and I love to help others accomplish tasks. I seek love through touch and affirmations, and I give it through gifting people things and experiences. My passions are in history, geography, and sports, and I love to see the pinnacle of success. I cry at the blink of eye; I am the sappiest of all people, and I love a good romance story.

Medication

When it comes down to the nitty-gritty of processing these disorders, however, the realization is that I must take medication to help me regulate my moods. The pills help to a degree, but without them, I am a mess and unbearable to live with.

I also go to out-patient therapy with a licensed counselor. Early on, we saw each other weekly, but have since graduated to more time between appointments, sometimes three to four weeks. We talk and process my issues and beliefs, but we also use a technique called EMDR.

Retraining the Brain: EMDR

Eye Movement Desensitization and Reprocessing uses taps, clicks, or eye movements, along with belief and trauma processing to slowly retarget and retrain the brain. It can take a few sessions or months of sessions for it to completely work, but by following my therapist's fingers as I retell and process trauma I've experienced, I've been able to work through many horrible moments in my life that have helped to form the disorders I now have.

If you are in therapy and finding little success with conventional methods, I urge you to explore EMDR therapy and find a licensed therapist in your area. It may help you as it has me.

Tracking

Besides therapy, I also have some coping mechanisms that help get me through rough days and difficult times. I like to make lists and keep them in my calendar to help organize myself and set goals for the day or week.

I also have a mood tracker, *A Year in Pixels*, which helps me look for trends, identify troublesome areas, and talk about key points with my therapist. I find it soothing to read, color, and nap, and may do all three or any one of the chosen activities if I need to decompress or have a moment to myself.

Meditating

I also listen to meditations when I'm having trouble sleeping or calming down. I specifically like *HeadSpace*, but just finding a meditation system that works for you can help you zone out and keep in touch with your inner self.

Grounding

Finally, I try to ground myself when I feel the paralyzing fear of anxiety wrapping itself around me. Grounding yourself is a technique that involves becoming hyper-aware of your senses and what you can acutely see, feel, hear, smell, etc. at that moment, allowing you to free yourself from the fear that tends to paralyze those with anxiety.

61%

OF TEACHERS REPORTED THAT THE JOB IS "OFTEN" OR "ALWAYS" STRESSFUL

Strategies FOR COPING WITH DEPRESSION

I'm sharing all this because I know teaching is a high-stress job. It comes with high demands, lots of pressure from various stakeholders, and young lives held in the balance.

I'm not the only one who has suffered from depression, anxiety, fear, self-loathing, etc. I want to make sure that if you're reading this out there and feel like I'm telling your story, or even a piece of it, that you are not alone. It's time we erase the stigma, and it's time that we get help. It's time that we practice what we preach and that we reach out for assistance from those professionals around us. It's time that we do what we need to do to be happy and healthy.

Menta health is just as important, if not more so than physical health. Take your sick days, use them for whatever type of health you need to improve, and be the best you that you can possibly be.

FOR MORE INSIGHT FROM BRITTANY, VISIT THECOLORADOCLASSROOM.COM

For me that meant quitting teaching. I had to walk away from the job I was meant for and the job I loved, to do what was right for me and my mental health. I was having daily migraines, panic and anxiety attacks, and was in tears on a regular basis. I knew I needed to re-approach my primary care physician and therapist and do a deep dive into my mental health and self-care. I started seeing a psychologist that controlled my medications and oversaw my treatment, and I switched therapists, not once, but twice, until I found what I needed in terms of treatment methods and care. It also means that I advocate and support others who are going through this same ordeal. I am here to talk, process, share, and give advice.

I am not a licensed therapist, psychologist, or doctor, and I can't tell you what's right for you, but if you find yourself unhappy, worried, or lost all the time, there are ways to get help and find that part of you that you miss. Talk to your PCP or use *Psychology Today* to find a local counselor or therapist that's right for you. You can get help and start living again.

I invite you to engage in a healthy conversation. Ask questions, seek advice, and share your story.

Empowering Students with Disabilities by CREATIVELY Bridging the Employment Gap

Olivia Rose Martins

Only 44% of adults with intellectual disabilities are in the work force, compared to 83% of adults without disabilities.

Olivia Rose Martins' drive to improve her students' future has led her to develop a unique new formula:

A crafty endeavor
+
some newly found business skills
+
a passion for empowering special ed students
=
a handmade doormat shop that seamlessly teaches economics while setting students up for a career option that is designed for their own success.

Unemployment rates for adults with developmental disabilities are more than twice as high as the average.

MEET
Olivia Rose

As a teacher, my first priority is to educate, inspire, and cultivate an environment where learning can happen in my classroom. In order to do that, I need to prioritize my own self-care outside of the classroom. In my life, self-care has many faces. It's working out, taking a long shower, watching TV, and listening to music, but most importantly, it's making and creating. In the most recent years, that has been through my online shop, *Olivia Rose Shoppe*, where I make and sell doormats. Allowing myself to dive into a world of creativity gives me a sense of well being and refreshment. In turn, I am able to create a positive environment for my students.

I come from a large family of 9 kids! Being the third, and the oldest girl instilled in me the leadership qualities that have allowed me to be successful in life and as a teacher. I LOVE to work out! In college, I trained for and ran two full marathons. I've lived in Florida almost my entire life. That means the beach is my happy place. I have horrible handwriting, so most of the time I use stencils for my work.

I've wanted to work with people with disabilities ever since I can remember! My favorite part about going to work every day is that I am finally doing what I have always wanted to do.

I've never labeled myself as 'creative' until recently. When I think of the word 'creative,' I automatically think of someone who can draw, paint, or produce a video or movie. I am the furthest from that. I don't even have good handwriting; how can I be labeled as creative!?

Yet, looking back on my life, creativity has always been an outlet for me. That's the beauty of creativity. It looks different to each individual person. I cannot draw, yet I love to put together and make my own face masks. I can't paint a landscape portrait, but I can use watercolors to make my own thank you notes.

To me, creativity has been more of a tinker process than an expressive emotional process. My creativity stems from different items I see as useful and discovering how I can make them in my own way. I guess that leads into how these doormats, as random as they are, really epitomize the creativity that I possess.

My passion has always been to work with those who have intellectual and developmental disabilities. "Special education teacher" was my sole answer to the whole "What do you want to be when you grow up" question everyone throws at you. In my young brain, it was the simplest way that I could work hands-on with people who had disabilities.

As I got to college, answering that question throughout my whole life was solidified when I absolutely knew that working with those with disabilities was where I was meant to be. Through the college process, I realized that secondary education (middle and high

Stats from Special Olympics

That's the beauty of creativity. It looks different to each individual person.

Her
CRAFT

school) was what I enjoyed most, especially high school, where students were about to graduate and really needed to focus on those independent living skills and what comes next for them.

There was a time between my undergrad and graduate school year that I became so antsy with life. I was annoyed that I had to keep taking classes just to do what I always wanted to do and aggravated at the time I spent creating lessons for fake students. All I wanted to do was be in charge of real ones: to love, cherish, and empower my own group of angels. Yet, I had to be patient... and in stress and boredom, my creativity flourishes.

Thus, *Olivia Rose Shoppe* was born. In that time of angst, I was able to realize that the future was mine, and if I wanted this, I needed to start it now. I started my shop by painting simple designs: a wooden plaque here, and a coffee mug there, just allowing myself to build something for the future. It wasn't until I took a psychology career counseling class that it clicked. My passion of helping those with disabilities did not have to be limited to being solely a teacher forever.

Olivia Rose Shoppe quickly turned into an outlet for me to help decrease the gap between those with disabilities and paying jobs. In the midst of this, I found a craft that I loved and was simple enough to teach my students - painting doormats. I then was able to implement a unit into my lesson plans that combined economic standards with financial literacy, and allow my students to dive into my creative world (and for my selfish reasons, see whether this could really work).

Fast forward 2 years... I am now teaching a more in depth unit called *Creating a Business,* and my students have now funded their own fun field trip. The entire process of creating my shop and combining my two passions has not been an easy one. I have gotten discouraged, messed up, and at times thought that I was completely crazy for even thinking I would be successful. *Olivia Rose Shoppe* is not yet where I had intended it to be, but I know that it will continue to grow. I continue to push because these kiddos deserve to have a fighting chance for a job and career as much as I did.

The doormats are quite simple to make, actually. The first step is creating a design online. This step usually takes me the longest. I tinker, gather ideas, and continually move around designs on my screen until they fully come together. The next step is ensuring my design is measured properly, then printing it out. After printing out my stencil, I use it to paint directly on each mat! Although the stencil allows me to be accurate in my designs for the mats, there is always paint to touch up to finish a design after the stencil is taken off.

I continue to carve out the time because of the future success. I think allowing myself to dream and create an image of what I want this business to look like in the future drives me most, knowing that if I work hard now, it will pay off in the long run. It's not always easy though. Most of the time, I am making mats and doing my shop related duties after a long day at work or on the weekends.

If you are a creative soul, but have a busy life as a teacher, don't focus on the limited time. Often, when I get stressed, pressed for time, or realize that I have no time left for myself, I begin to dwell on the amount of time that I don't have. Instead, I have now begun to look at it in the opposite way. How much time DO I have? I DO have 5 minutes to pull up my graphics and mess around. I DO have 3 extra minutes in the store to get some supplies. Since much of my life does not normally revolve around creativity, it is easier for me to enjoy those few minutes when I look at it as a gift rather than a lack of time.

For me, the trickiest part has been the behind the scenes of everything. Learning how to run a business, marketing, finances, and everything else I've done is self-taught, from Instagram pictures to purchasing large orders of mats. I think that is what most people don't realize about a creative business. The creativity comes easily, whereas the management and making sure this whole idea stays afloat is the more difficult part.

Her
MISSION

The mission of Olivia Rose Shoppe is to lower the percentage of those with disabilities who are unemployed.

Currently, that looks like completing orders on my own, and saving all the money made in the shop for the goal of opening a brick and mortar store to employ those with disabilities, all while teaching my classroom students employment skills. In the future, I hope for *Olivia Rose Shoppe* to be a business that employs those with disabilities and equips them with job skills needed to be successful in the working environment.

My students impact each decision I make. Are they behaving right for me to teach? Do they understand what I am teaching? Are they able to interact with my lesson? Each decision that I make at school is solely based on the students and their betterment.

There is a definite positive and negative to planning lessons in the area of Special Education. The negative is that there is no one single curriculum that works for all of your students, nor is there a learning level that all of your students are on. Yet, that also becomes the positive. Due to that fact, special education teachers are able to be creative in the ways that they create and present their lessons.

I love this opportunity for creativity in all of my lessons. It also is what allows me to teach my students through creating and running a business. The economic class that I teach has standards that are focused on business creation, management, marketing, supply, demand, and financial literacy. After I have taught all of the concrete items, the students get to put their learning to use by running their business of painting doormats. *Olivia Rose Shoppe* is able to combine with my lessons for student success.

I once received a card from a student's mother. She wrote "Thank you for loving on Student X this year. You have made her feel valued and that her life matters, and for that, I am forever grateful".

I want all teachers to know that they are valued. The work that they are doing whether they feel like a success or a failure, is being appreciated. You are truly giving meaning to each student each morning when you look at them, say good morning and continue to give yourself to them. You are teaching them that they are important and that they matter no matter what.

TEACHER TIPS TO TRY
from Olivia Rose

x x x x x x x x x x x x x x x x x x x x x x x x x x

5 tips for walking through Target when you don't want to spend any more money:

1. Remind yourself that you don't need to spend any more money on your students... even if it is in the $3 section.

2. Head down. Walk straight past the office supplies. You do NOT need any more pens.

3. No, a new coffee mug for school will not help you teach better tomorrow.

4. Don't even DARE make eye contact with the *Hearth and Soul* section. Nope, not even a glance!

5. It's not real money when you buy wine.

Meditation in the classroom:

The first thing my self-contained class does in the morning is our meditation. It's nothing specific at all. Some days it is piano music, and other days it is a talking meditation.

It allows the class as a whole to settle in. For myself, it forces me to take that time to take a breath before the day starts. For my students, it allows them to actually stop.

Many of them are so excited and constantly talking and moving throughout the day. A few moments of meditation allows the students to notice the difference between calm and all the other emotions going on inside.

SUPPORT THE MISSION

Follow @oliviaroseshoppe on Instagram or shop for doormats for your home and classroom at Oliviaroseshoppe on Etsy.

DIY steam room - for all of my self-care lovers out there:

>> Grab a bottle of your favorite essential oils. (I recommend lavender for this.)
>> Spritz your shower walls with the essential oil.
>> Turn your shower on as hot as it can go. Leave the bathroom (with the fan off), and close the door for about 3-5 minutes.
>> After 5 minutes, you will walk back into a relaxing DIY sauna smelling of your favorite oils, ready for a relaxing shower!

a positive twist

COMPLAINING ABOUT SCHOOL:
We've all been there (probably even within the past 24 hours!). You may make excuses, like, "Venting is healthy," but there is a huge difference between positive and negative venting, and you just may be heightening the problem and any accompanying anxiety. Instead, in the spirit of working toward gratitude, positivity, and progress, try out these more assertive approaches that help twist a challenging situation from negative to positive.
by Kelly Barendt

ADMIN

lacking in backup

SITUATION
"My principal and I don't share the same behavior management beliefs. When a student is disrespectful or a serious problem in the classroom, I can't send them to the principal's office, because she won't provide a reasonable consequence. Other teachers feel the same way."

SOLUTION
Whether or not your principal is being intentional, she is sending an important message. When it comes to disciplining students, it is up to you. Take this as a signal that you can handle it well on your own. Devise a plan with other teachers. If a student needs to be removed send him or her to a different classroom (preferably a different grade level) until that teacher is ready to send the student back. Be clear, consistent, and unafraid to call students' parents when problems occur. This removes the responsibility of providing consequences from your principal.

killing the good vibes

SITUATION
"My teammates and I feel my principal is promoting a negative school culture. He frequently puts teachers down, criticizes teaching practices, and to top it all off, doesn't take time to get to know us or our classes. I know complaining isn't a productive solution to the problem, but we are all scared to talk to him, and feel like we have nowhere to turn."

SOLUTION
You're right, complaining with co-workers only serves to increase tensions. If you need to vent, do so with a partner or friend outside of school, and only for a brief amount of time. Replaying conflicts in your head takes up too much time and energy; you need to move into problem-solving mode as soon as you can. Next, as long as your principal isn't directly interfering with your ability to teach, try the classic approach of "killing him with kindness." You need to remain positive and professional on your end. If your principal doesn't even do as much as make eye contact in the morning, brightly (and without sarcasm) say, "Good Morning Mr._____!" Most people will come around to your positivity, but if not, you are doing the right thing and being the bigger person. If he is directly affecting your teaching, call your union representative. Otherwise, show the teaching staff by example that as a team, you can overcome this and set the tone yourselves. Lead the much needed morale boost yourself.

unfair advantages for athletes

SITUATION
"The high school where I teach really values our sports teams and goes to great lengths to support students who are athletes. My principal wants us to give student athletes special treatment, like excusing them for being tardy to class or allowing them to turn papers in late. This goes against my teaching philosophy; it's unfair to students who do not play school sports."

SOLUTION
I might encourage you to ask for forgiveness, not permission here. Set your own class policies at the start of the school year. Clearly explain and document on a class syllabus that you will not accept late work from any student, and why. Explain that you care about each and every student and believe they should all be treated equally and with respect. Do what you know is best, and if you are met with backlash, politely refer back to the agreed upon syllabus. If the principal gets involved, politely, but assertively explain how providing special treatment for certain students goes against your philosophy of teaching. Keep it focused on what is best for the students, and reiterate that you are teaching responsibility, priorities, discipline, etc. in cooperation with their athletic goals.

PARENTS

never off the clock

SITUATION
"Parents contact me at any hour of the day or night for inconsequential reasons. Don't they realize I'm teaching their child during the day, and need to get some sleep at night? I understand and appreciate the concern they have for their child, but sometimes it's just too much. They won't leave me alone!"

SOLUTION
This year, you may have to accept being in ninja mode and keep trying to master your evasive tactics. But next year, set expectations at the beginning of the school year during parent-teacher night or a note home. Point out the fact that you appreciate and share their love and concern for their child, but need to set boundaries so that you can be the best teacher you can be. If you choose to give your phone number, be clear that it should only be used before 9:00 p.m. (or whatever time you choose). Explain that you teach all day, and need to give your full attention to the children, so if they call and leave a message, you will get back to them as soon as possible. Give them alternate points of access for urgent situations (through the office) and clear guidelines on what methods of communication are best for different scenarios. Most parents will be understanding, but unfortunately there may be some that just don't get it. In those cases, you need to clearly set your own boundaries. Don't respond to emails, calls, or texts after your agreed upon time. To keep your sanity during off hours, don't even check your inbox.

(faking?) flying blind

SITUATION
"I never received a response from one of my 4th grader's parents about the child's slipping grades, even though I reached out many times via email, phone calls and voicemails, and notes home. Then, when conferences came around the parents were appalled and angry with me for not informing them beforehand. How do I prevent similar situations from happening again with other parents in the future?"

SOLUTION
Document. Document. Document. You sent a note home on December 5th asking for a parent signature, but never received one? You called mom on December 12th, and left a voicemail, but never got a call back? Document every instance in detail, and carbon copy administrators as needed so you can relax and know you can show where the accountability lies. In future cases, once you start to recognize a pattern, get your principal involved. Sometimes, a message from the principal creates more alarm and urgency in parents.

mother knows best

SITUATION
"The parent of one of my 6th grade students is a current math teacher in a neighboring district. Her district takes a different approach to teaching certain Pre-Algebra concepts, and she thinks my approach is wrong and hurting her child in the long run."

SOLUTION
Set up a meeting with the parent, and invite your math coach (if you have one), for a polite and civil conversation about the curriculum and your differing approaches to teaching and learning. Be prepared with research that backs up your own approach. Be careful you don't condemn or "gang up" on the parent. The purpose of this meeting is for each to understand where the other one is coming from, not to criticize or put anyone down. To make this a positive encounter, focus on being a good listener. This mother wants to share what she is passionate about! Let her show and tell you all the reasons that she feels so strongly about the math strategies she teaches. Once she feels heard, she is likely to be relieved that you are at least keeping her thoughts in mind and working to incorporate the best of both worlds (as you see fit). Discuss a variety of points, like the research backing up the methods and ways teachers incorporate the methods. Finally, genuinely ask and discuss, "Is there a way we can reach a compromise?" Whether or not you decide to teach both methods, or stick to your guns, you'll have shown your willingness to hear her out, and hopefully bond over your shared passion for your content.

solve problems by making your own silver lining

STUDENTS

wasting my breath

SITUATION
"I have a wonderful class of 8th graders for third period Geometry, except one or two students are extremely inattentive. Their behavior isn't necessarily "bad," it just appears they are not trying to focus. I often catch them playing on their phones or daydreaming in the middle of class. Of course, everyone does this from time to time, but this happens everyday, if not multiple times a class."

SOLUTION
Oftentimes, when students are inattentive, the lesson is either too challenging or not challenging enough. A great, proactive strategy is to implement engaging activities in your lessons. Try things like playing educational geometry games, using math manipulatives, or closely monitoring small groups that require participation. These will naturally prevent disengagement. Another idea is to implement "minute papers." At the end of class, give your students one minute to answer the following questions:

- Today I learned...
- I was surprised to realize...
- My biggest question is...
- I'm still confused about...

Then, give the class one minute to share with a partner.

You'll be able to see whether or not the students can answer these and recap the lesson. If these strategies do not work, it may be worth communicating with the student, individually. If the student is nodding off during class, there may be a deeper issue going on, like lack of sleep, a poor diet, or some other stressor at home. If you can get to the bottom of it, you'll be setting the student up for success in more ways than you realize, since this behavior is likely impacting them in other rooms as well.

pushing the limit

SITUATION
"A 10th grade student of mine is driving me crazy! He's what you would label a "class clown", but he doesn't know when to stop. He also doesn't seem to have a filter, and can quickly cross the line from silly and light-hearted to downright crude and inappropriate. How should I handle this student?"

SOLUTION
I'm not normally one to recommend ever publicly disciplining a student, but it sounds like it's necessary in this case. This student, as well as the rest of the class, needs to know this behavior is unacceptable and will not be tolerated. Be proactive and set this expectation right away, before the behavior develops into a serious problem. If you realize it's too late, and you are in over your head, call the parents, student, and admin together to officially prescribe a hard reset, with a starting date immediately following the meeting. Be clear that he has a blank slate that comes along with a very high standard. Set up a zero tolerance policy going forward, and make sure you do not let even one incident slip.

social anxiety

SITUATION
"One of my 2nd grade girls is painfully shy. She's such a sweetheart, but refuses to make eye contact, always keeps to herself, and never says more than a few whispers. How do I pull her out of her shell?"

SOLUTION
Handle this situation delicately with patient baby steps. Don't pressure her to speak in front of the class. When you're speaking 1-on-1, try to get her to repeat what you just said. Praise her! Another strategy is to use fellow classmates to help. Many kids will naturally help, but try pairing her with a kind student for a long time to help her feel comfortable.

HOME & FAMILY

mental load

SITUATION
"School has really been weighing on me, lately. I feel the administration is asking too much, we are under equipped, and my students are out of control. I am so stressed and I am unleashing it on my family. I lash out at my husband and kids when they definitely don't deserve it. Everyone can see I'm just not my normal, joyful self. What should I do?"

SOLUTION
The emotional weight of teaching is heavier than many people realize. Worrying about our students keeps us up at night. Our hearts are so invested, yet the job is overwhelming and filled with frustrations. Try things like regular exercise and meditation. Try positive and assertive solutions to everyday problems (like the ones mentioned here). If time goes by and none of this helps, it might be time to move to a new school. It might sound overwhelming and scary, but there are school environments that support happy, healthy teachers. Remember the saying, You can't pour from an empty cup. You need to take care of yourself and your family, first and foremost. If your job isn't fulfilling and you're unhappy day in and day out, you might need to change your surroundings. An underlying tension can build up to make for a very unhealthy lifestyle. Find your own positive solution, and make sure to continue to re-evaluate periodically.

too drained for chores

SITUATION
"My husband gets home from work a few hours after I do, and wonders why the house is a mess, there are dishes in the sink, piles of dirty laundry, and dinner isn't started. I am exhausted at this point, and he just doesn't understand; he thinks I was just hanging out with teenagers all day. I've tried to explain the amount of effort that goes into teaching, but he doesn't get it."

SOLUTION
It's difficult for non-teachers to truly understand the job of a teacher; many think they understand because they went to school, but we know there's so much more that goes on behind the scenes. Ask your spouse to volunteer in your classroom for a day, or even a couple of hours, to get a fresh perspective of the work involved. Talk about his own work frustrations so you can both gain perspective. Show each other appreciation. It goes both ways. Finding a fellow teacher friend can be an excellent way to share the joys and struggles of teaching.

endless homework

SITUATION
"I know all teachers have this problem, but I seriously feel like my workload is neverending! I can't help but bring my work home, and continue working through the evening. I'm grading papers on the couch, lesson planning at the kitchen table after dinner, and later, communicating with parents while I should be relaxing with my husband."

SOLUTION
First, prioritize. What is most important to you? Things like redoing your classroom bulletin board or creating a perfect detailed presentation for tomorrow's lesson, or things like grading students' papers for a state assessment with an approaching deadline? Think about what you absolutely need to do and what can wait or will be okay if done in a rush or not done at all. If it absolutely cannot wait until tomorrow, take it home with you. Next, set up a designated area in your home for work, and set a timer for 30, 45, 60 minutes, whatever is appropriate, and complete your work, distraction-free, until the timer goes off. Then, quit. Whether you accomplished your goals for the day or not, you need to set a limit. You will never feel caught up, but this way you know you have focused fully for a reasonable amount of time. Cutting out distractions improves productivity for the set time period, and then when you're with your family you can give them your full attention.

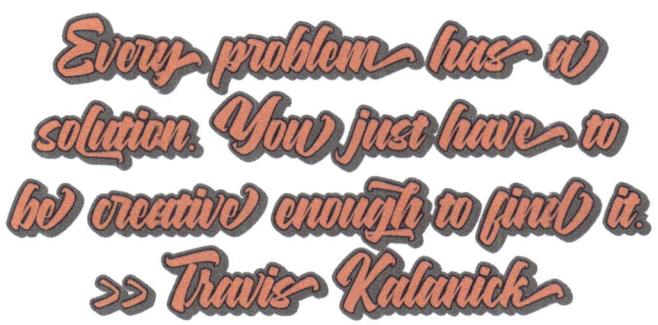

Every problem has a solution. You just have to be creative enough to find it. >> Travis Kalanick

creative classroom CORNERS

Don't let the empty corners of your classroom go to waste. Use these inspiring ideas to ignite your creative spark and help you use every bit of space you have.

The music room can sometimes be loud and overwhelming. My calm corner is a place for students to take a moment of peace if they need to in this environment.

How Students Use the Area:
Students go to the corner if they are feeling angry, overwhelmed, or sad. Older students come and go as needed, and younger students have a secret signal they ask me with.

What to Include:
journal, puzzles, stress balls, timer, and lots of textured items

@annacwiles

the calm down corner

This corner of our classroom is referred to as our Classroom Cafe. Its purpose is to provide students with flexible seating options during our independent work time.

How Students Use the Area:
My kids use this corner every day to engage in stations, collaborative activities and independent work.

What to Include:
In our Classroom Cafe corner you can find a high top table, two bar stools, cozy floor pillows and an illuminated tree. The table and stools were purchased at a local thrift shop and turned into my summer DIY project, as I worked to give them a rustic appearance.

@teachingbooksmarts

the classroom cafe corner

the conflict corner

This corner is a space for peace and calm, where children can be away from the hustle and bustle of the classroom and listen to their own hearts and minds. They can also use the space for quiet conversations with friends and are invited to use the space for conflict resolution.

What to Include:
- Scarves
- Mirrors
- Plants
- Feathers
- Books about feelings
- A kaleidoscope
- Dolls

@tinkertots.my

the plant corner

I use live plants and books to help expose the children to things that are important for development and stimulation, but also found less frequently at home.

How Students Use the Area:
Students can borrow books and magazines, and interact with the plants. Both plants were named by students, and many of the books are worth AR points as an added bonus.

What to Include:
In my corner I have a small bookcase loaded with books focused on math and science. On top of the bookshelf is a vine named "Snivey" by the class, and on a desk next to it is a fern named "Bernie." There are also flower and insect posters on the walls.

@toristory10

The zen tent is part of the cool down corner in the Promise Room. The Promise Room classroom is used for K-5 students who need a break to facilitate the 3R process of rest, recover, and return to class. The zen tent evolved from watching YogaFoster.com webinars and was inspired by their zen den idea. They are a wonderful resource for teachers looking to incorporate mindfulness and yoga into the classroom.

How Students Use the Area:
Students relax in the tent while discussing what made them upset, process emotions, and brainstorm how to make it right. They enjoy the calming and restorative textures of the plush chairs, pillows, and poufs. The interactive floor tiles that run along the sink counter are fun and can be rearranged in different formations.

What to Include:
plush chairs
tent
air mattress
faux fur throw
soft body pillows (animal print)
owl pillow
soft poufs
toys for creative play
interactive floor tiles

@elfinwear

the zen tent

This Calming Corner is located in my office, which is just off the cafeteria in our school. As the School Counselor, I use this corner for de-escalation and teaching relaxation skills.

How Students Use the Area:
Students who come into my office to calm down gravitate to the puppets and soft toys. They also love the flip sequin pillow.

What to Include:
I have milk crates with chair cushion covers, a basket of puppets and stuffed animals, glitter filled calm-down bottles, and other tactile items.

@eagletschoolcounselor

the counselor's corner

the latinx corner

This corner was inspired by the Latinx culture. As a Spanish teacher, I want to expose my students to the things we will be learning in class.

How Students Use the Area:
This corner is used to make my students curious about Latinx culture. I want them to ask questions about Day of the Dead, Frida Kahlo, and the guiro.

What to Include:
Day of the Dead pillow, "Mi casa es su casa" pillow, 2 ceramic llamas, guiro instrument, ceramic Day of the Dead skull, Frida Kahlo poster, sarape, 2 sombreros and a map of America.

@maestramoctez

POSITIVE

Do you ever find yourself struggling to find enough positive comments for certain students' report cards? It's not only a matter of tactful phrasing, it's a process of truly seeking out the beauty in each child. We've lined up some characteristics of "challenging" student behaviors with positive traits that can often accompany them.

Even if some of these features prevent a student from staying focused, or bring you frustration in class, there are benefits to every type of personality, and beauty in every student's soul.

Here is some help for finding that positive twist for each child.

Save this list!

COMMENTS

made easy

It's normal to get stumped on some students when trying to write positive report card comments! This can happen with certain kids if their personalities do not mesh with the standard "good student" characteristics.

Every student does bring something special to the class, so we've provided a list of suggestions for positive characteristics that you can use to describe kids with more challenging traits.

It's especially important to show the student that you see these deeper, hidden attributes. You'll also show the parents that you see and value those great things about their kid, particularly since it's possible that in past years, teachers have sometimes overlooked the positive side. Hopefully, this list helps you adjust your perspective to find the blessings within each child's personality.

*Note: These are only suggestions to highlight the student's strengths. These are not meant to replace addressing any problems in the classroom. Also, only use the suggested comments that are actually true about the individual student. Everyone is unique!

TRAITS THAT MAY APPLY:

If this student's challenges in the classroom include...	... then consider whether this positive twist is accurate / a good fit. (These can often accompany this particular challenge.)
talkative during class	enthusiastic about being at school
not on task	creative / imaginative
conflicts with classmates	cares deeply about relationships with classmates
shouts out answers	excited to learn and share
bossy	takes charge / natural leader
doesn't work well in groups	a different way of looking at things / self-reliant
shy	peaceful spirit / calm and well-mannered
asks too many questions	inquisitive mind
disorganized	sense of adventure / unique approaches
does not speak up in class	listens attentively
doodles and draws	artistic and creative
class clown	confident with a sense of humor
clueless / spaced out	curious / dreamer
tendency to be overdramatic	self-assured / expressive
nerdy / social difficulties	driven by specific interests / focused
cries frequently	thoughtful / sensitive nature
not comfortable in social situations	hard working / introspective

OTHER POSITIVE CHARACTERISTICS TO CONSIDER:

Creativity
Sense of humor
Sense of adventure
Willingness to try
Inquisitive mind
Unique personality
Cheerful attitude
Persistence
Leadership ability
Internal strength
Loving spirit

Bravery
Resilience
Integrity
Fun personality
Friendliness
Unique perspective
Peaceful spirit
Thoughtfulness
Self-confidence
Respectful attitude
Enthusiasm

Dependability
Self-reliance
Curiosity
Expressiveness
Self-control
Social skills
Maturity
Cooperative attitude
Empathy
Independence
Pleasant attitude

Ambition
Efficient attitude
Playful spirit
Generosity
Sensitive nature
Patience
Hard-working
Different way of looking at the world
Willingness to accept a challenge

playing with shapes, scents, and textures

MAKING YOUR OWN ORGANIC

SOAP

photos and soap bars by janice wan

>> *elementary teacher*
>> *soap maker*
>> *lifestyle vlogger*

getting crafty

WHY DELVE INTO SOAP MAKING AS A HOBBY?

Making handmade soap batches is a fun way to get creative, but also offers a practical result. You'll even cut down on waste and packaging, and possibly save money. An hour's work can set you up with a stock of soap that lasts for months.

More importantly, you'll know the ingredients. Unlike standard soaps you purchase, you can know that your blend has no added synthetic dyes, fragrances, or additives. You'll be able to customize your batch with your favorite scent, test out fun shapes, and find your perfect level of exfoliation.

As an added bonus, you can keep the glycerin in your soap. Companies often extract this byproduct to sell it separately, since it is valuable on its own. But glycerin is an emollient that has moisturizing benefits. When you make your own soap, you can ensure that the glycerin is still in there to soften and smooth your skin.

Handmade soaps make wonderful gifts as well!

THE BASICS

  Heat a simple soap base. You can purchase pre-made cubes that are ready to melt, and then just use a normal kitchen pot and medium heat on the stove. (A microwave will work too.) Or, if you want to get more ambitious, you can make your soap base from scratch. If you do blend your own recipe with glycerin, oil, and lye you'll have to be careful, since lye is caustic. Do your research if you make your own instead of purchasing melt-and-pour cubes that have already been through the saponification process. Either way, choose natural ingredients like avocado oil or sunflower oil, shea butter, and coconut oil.

  Mix in natural dyes to color your soap, essential oils to scent it, and any other ingredients that you'd like to include. Try flower petals and soothing scents for a bath bar, or citrus and herbs in a kitchen soap. If you are adding texture to make your soap an exfoliant, add the other ingredients first, then let it cool for a few moments before adding the exfoliating ingredients. This will help them blend evenly instead of sinking to the bottom. Poppyseeds, coarse salt, coffee grounds, and oatmeal give a great texture and strong scrubbing power. Play with different creative combinations that you think will work well together!

  Carefully pour your liquid soap into a mold. You can use a silicone cake pan, ice cube trays, or even a shaped mold. Spray the top with rubbing alcohol. Let the soap cool on the countertop for a few hours, or in the refrigerator for an hour. (If you opt to use lye and do the saponification process yourself, it takes much longer.) Once it's cool, you can remove the soap from the trays or molds and use it right away! If you use a large loaf pan, you can blend beautiful swirls into the liquid soap and then slice it into bars once it cools. Use a vegetable peeler to smooth off the edges if needed.

CREATIVE BLENDS

All of these bars begin with a soap base formula of olive oil, coconut oil, shea butter, avocado oil, castor oil, lye, and glycerin. But teacher and soap maker Janice Wan has spent many of her "Soaping Sundays" testing new ingredient combinations to perfect these special bars. She likes to play with different scents and colors, and adds a variety of interesting exfoliants.

Janice explains that these elements in her base soap bar recipe make it "the perfect elixir for any skin type. Ingredients are all natural, so it's perfectly gentle for sensitive skin types. Five different types of oils, all targeting different skin needs are thoughtfully mixed together to hydrate and moisturize dry skin, which is an added plus for teachers because we are constantly washing and working with our hands."

From there, she adds to the base. " Some soap batches are topped with lavender buds, calendula petals, rose petals, poppy seeds, or oatmeal to add a gentle exfoliating effect. Upon pouring a newly made batch of soap into its mold, beautiful swirled designs can be created using a spoon or stick to give the soap bars texture. When it comes to scents, I like to think of soap making like baking—just no licking and taste-tasting along the way, please! I find a lot of inspiration through the ingredients that are used to make popular pastries or food recipes. More often than not, the scents of those food ingredients pair very well together. For example, vanilla pumpkin spice sounds delectable and seems like a very realistic dessert that many people would enjoy eating. Why not find a pumpkin spice fragrance oil and combine it with a warm vanilla fragrance oil? I thought of combining those two scents and ended up making one of my husband's favorite soap bars!"

Try these combinations that our expert soapmaker, Janice has created, or use your own imagination to pull together a brand new blend.

Janice teaches 2nd grade, and shares: "As teachers, we have never-ending deadlines and to-do lists. We are constantly giving ourselves and pouring our hearts into others. It's hard not to lose ourselves in the process. Teachers are naturally givers and it's so important to set limits, slow down, take care of ourselves, and enjoy the little things in life. Being the best that we can be for our little learners and our own families starts with taking care of ourselves first. We must prioritize our mental and emotional health. For some, that might look like cozying up to a nice cup of coffee and a book, taking a long walk, grabbing dinner with friends, taking a bubble bath with a glass of Chardonnay, prioritizing a creative passion, or all of the above!

When I am taking time for myself and filling my cup, I find myself feeling much more energized and in a more positive head space to tackle a new day in the classroom with my sweet little learners. We live in a world with never-ending deadlines and to-do lists; it's so hard not to get lost in the chaos of it all. It's so important to create a self-care ritual that allows you to slow down, take care of yourself, and enjoy the little things in life. I've always been passionate about skincare and self-care. I wanted to find a way where I could provide people with a relaxing experience to escape the stresses of the day. I knew that it needed to be something that people already do regularly and wouldn't require a lot of effort or investment of time.... SHOWERING!

I've always believed that self-care doesn't have to be something extravagant—it can be something as simple as choosing a nicely scented soap to decompress with in the shower and wash away the stresses of the day. I wanted to help people create a cost friendly spa-like retreat in their very own bathroom."

Activated charcoal is an ingredient in this soap bar and it has detoxifying properties-it draws bacteria, dirt, and impurities to the skin's surface, which helps purify your skin and achieve a flawless complexion. This soap is ideal for fighting acne.

charcoal + cologne scents

The Green Tea Soap Bar has a bright and crisp scent that will make your shower experience a refreshing one! This soap bar has hints of citrus, pear, green tea, and apples. It has a beautiful calming light green layer sitting atop a fluffy cream bottom layer.

*green tea
citrus scent
pear scent
apple scent
poppyseeds*

jasmine scent
poppyseed
calendula petals

The jasmine flower is known for its beauty and fragrance. Like the flower, this soap bar is a beautiful work of art with gorgeous swirls of black and white topped off with poppy seeds and dainty calendula flowers.

cherry scent
rose petals
glitter

The sweetly fragrant Spring Cherry Blossom Soap Bar has a beautiful floral aroma that's reminiscent of cherry blossom flowers. This soap bar has a beautiful pink top and creamy white bottom, topped off with gorgeous crushed rose petals to give it the perfect aesthetic touch.

honeysuckle
poppyseeds
glitter
gold mica dust

The Honeysuckle Soap Bar will take you down a stroll on memory lane. This light fragrant aroma will trigger fond childhood memories of when we picked honeysuckles from their bushes. The scent is alluring and irresistible. The soap is a gorgeous creamy yellow with faint peach colored swirls.

lavender scent
exfoliating seeds

When the all-natural Lavender Bliss soap bar is used in a hot shower, the lavender scent gives you the most calming and relaxing experience, releasing tension in your tired muscles. Lavender essential oil has many skin care benefits like reducing redness, blotchiness, and acne.

This soap has a crisp citrus smell that will leave you feeling energized and ready to conquer the day! The soap is a creamy orange bar with a sprinkling of orange peels.

Where to Find Janice & her Soaps

Buy soap on Etsy: SoapandCoByJanice

YouTube: Janice Wan

Instagram: @lifebyjanice

JANICE'S 3 TIPS FOR SUCCESSFUL SOAP MAKING

1 >> Always wear gloves and safety goggles—get your chemistry 101 on!

2 >> Have your hair tied and pulled back—messy teacher bun preferred.

3 >> As with teaching, don't be afraid to fail! Not all soap batches will turn out successful! I can't even begin to tell you how many failed batches I've made. ;)

SPICE UP YOUR SOAPS

The real joy of making it yourself is being able to make your soap more special than what you can find at the store. Try these fun and crafty soap hacks to give your new bar a twist.

Hide a Treasure Inside

Before the soap is set aside to cool, place a special item inside. This works well for gift soap, or is a fun surprise for kids using the soap. They can reveal a small metal trinket, money, or a little animal toy as they scrub. A piece of jewelry is another fun option that can be customized for a gift. For adults, you can embed a crystal in the bar, and even leave a portion of it poking out.

Additions to try:
shredded coconut, sugar, aloe vera, matcha powder, coffee beans, clay, beeswax, cinnamon, citrus zest, chia seeds, dried herbs, oatmeal, honey, flower petals, mint, silk fibers, coarse salt, goat milk, calendula or lavender flowers

Embed Practicality

Try making soap "pops" for youngsters by molding your bars in ice pop molds and adding sticks or handles. A rope loop or a stick will help keep the wet soap from slipping away! Another way to make your soap practical is to slice up a natural loofah sponge into large "coins" and embed a slice into each piece. Ensure that it fills the piece of soap, going all the way to the edge of the mold, so the soap just barely coats the loofah. This will give you a small soap-soaked piece of the sponge that suds and scrubs in one step.

Play with Shapes

Silicone ice cube trays make wonderful molds for small, individual sized soaps. But you can also try making your soap in a thin layer on a deep cookie sheet or a cake pan (Grease it first). Then, you'll be able to stamp out pieces by cutting the soap into shapes once it has hardened. Mini fondant cutters are perfect for this, and come in a variety of fun sizes and shapes, even including letters and numbers!

Abundance through *Simplicity*

HOW MINIMALISM CAN LEAD TO FINDING GRATITUDE

RECOMMENDED APP: "TOSS" FOR EASY DECLUTTERING

BY MICHAELA BACKLUND

For many years, I was admittedly someone who was always searching for "more". I think many people can relate to this feeling. "If I have more money, I'll be happier. If I can update my kitchen, I'll be content in my home. If we go on this vacation, I won't be stressed anymore..."

About a year ago, my husband gifted me a gratitude journal. At first, coming up with things to be grateful for was difficult. I would write about basic things, such as my family, a home, and a good job. Eventually, I began to dig deeper into what truly brought me joy in my daily life, simple things that brought me joy, maybe even without me noticing it. I began to realize when small things brought me joy, in the moment. It was things like sitting on the couch and smelling the candle scent coming from the kitchen table, or the excitement of starting a new novel.

I began to recognize these feelings, and feel grateful for these small moments as they happened. The practice of gratitude began to carry over into my natural day to day life. Eventually, I realized that I was happier, less stressed, and truly grateful for the life that I have, and for each day that I get to be alive on this Earth. I began to feel lucky for all my blessings, instead of thinking about what else I wanted or could have.

My journey with minimalism is fairly new. After years of always feeling like I needed more, I had accumulated a lot of "stuff". I read Marie Kondo's book, *The Life Changing Magic of Tidying Up*, and was intrigued by her idea of only keeping items that spark joy. At first, it seemed a little silly to hold each item and ask myself, "does this make me feel joyful?" However, it was a strategy that made me realize how much I had in my home that I truly didn't care about!

For years, having a closet full of clothes or a kitchen filed with gadgets made me feel like I was getting closer to "having it all." Since starting my minimalism journey, I have donated, sold, or thrown away over 1,200 items from my home! Are my walls and drawers bare? No! However, each item and space in my home has a purpose. My house now feels like a home. It is a place that brings me calm, joy, and comfort.

YOU HAVE SUCCEEDED IN LIFE WHEN ALL YOU REALLY WANT IS ONLY WHAT YOU REALLY NEED. >> VERNON HOWARD

"IF I CAN UPDATE MY KITCHEN, I'LL BE CONTENT IN MY HOME. IF WE GO ON THIS VACATION, I WON'T BE STRESSED ANYMORE."

BALANCING WORK AND LIFE

Make your mental health a priority! You cannot be a good teacher if you are not in your best mindset because you're battling difficult emotions and stress. When your home life is in order, your work life will follow suit!

ADVICE FOR TEACHERS OF THE WORLD

Teachers have one of the most difficult and rewarding jobs in the world!! It is easy to become burnt out. Make teaching fun! Enjoy each day with your students and make the best out of difficult situations! Your first priority should be making sure students feel safe, respected and valued at school!

ADJUST YOUR PERSPECTIVE

One of my life mottos is to #ComplainLess! When we complain about what isn't going right, things we wish were different, or ways our lives are difficult, this takes a toll on our mindset and mental health. Change your perspective! Practicing gratitude will train your mind to automatically think more positively!

Especially during difficult circumstances, the first step to developing a more positive mindset is to become aware of any negative thoughts. Try to become conscious of these moments, and then learn to interrupt them by practicing gratitude! When you catch yourself complaining, stop to think of three reasons your life is good!

minimize

I am in my fourth year of teaching first grade. I have a passion for early literacy and engaging, high quality children's books!

I am married (to a teacher!) and have two dogs. I am also pregnant with my first child! I am beyond excited to share my love of books, music, and adventure with our child. Expecting our first child has been a huge inspiration to live a life with more joy and gratitude!

GETTING STARTED WITH MINIMALISM AT HOME

Minimalism does not mean getting rid of everything and living in a tiny home. When I began practicing minimalism, this is what many family members and friends thought. Minimalism can mean many different things to different people. My home still has pictures on the walls, shelves filled with books, and a nursery filled with toys.

Minimalism is realizing what items in your home bring you joy and serve a purpose. It is being intentional about the physical items you allow in your space and environments!

When beginning to declutter your home, it can be very difficult to commit to getting rid of your things! Start with one space at a time, such as one kitchen cupboard, and only keep what you use often inside the cupboard. Place everything else in a box and hide it away for a month. Set an alarm on your phone or write it in your calendar! Go back to this box after a month and re-evaluate. Did you miss anything in this box? Did you even notice that these items were gone? No? Time to sell, donate, or toss!

Start small! Begin with one cupboard and don't start another until you've completed it! I like to take everything out so that I can thoroughly evaluate each item. If you haven't used the item in the last year, donate, toss, or sell. For items that you're having difficulty letting go of, get a box and store those items away for a month. Set an alarm on your phone or write it in your calendar. After a month, re-evaluate each of these items. Did you miss it? Did you need it? Did you even notice it was gone? Downsizing and simplifying your space is a process. It cannot be done in a day. Keep this is mind!

When simplifying your wardrobe, take every clothing item you have out of your closet, dresser, etc. Make a big pile! Take each item, one at a time, and hold it up. Have you worn it in the last year? Do you really love this piece of clothing? Is it versatile? Place clothes that you know you are ready to let go of in a box. Clothing items you are unsure of, set to the side. When you finish, put away the "keep items". Try on each of the items you are unsure of and re-evaluate. If you don't love that piece of clothing, or it doesn't serve a specific purpose, then toss, sell, or donate!!

MINIMALISM IN THE CLASSROOM

Children do not expect extravagant lessons and over the top "Instagram worthy" classrooms at school. They also do not expect the ten different writing templates that you've provided them for writer's workshop. One way that I keep things simple in my classroom is by letting students explore with BLANK paper to create, design, and write. This applies to all subject areas! Not only does this save me a ton of time on Pinterest and at the copy machine, but my students are using their imagination, being creative, and given even MORE opportunity for choice!

Children just want to feel loved, valued, and appreciated. Focus your time on making that your priority! Instead of spending your valuable prep time creating perfect anchor charts to use, spend that time writing a thoughtful note to a handful of students, letting them know you are grateful for having them in your class! Your students will feel more valued and motivated to learn in your classroom, and in return, you will feel an overflowing sense of joy and gratitude!

You do not have to do it all. Simple is better, and often, less is more. Focus on one area, whether it's in your teaching or in your classroom, and be determined to make that one area better. I have found that taking baby steps is the key! My experience with trying to "do it all" only brought me stress, disappointment, and a lack of focus on my students.

We practice "Thankful Thursday" during our morning meetings. Each Thursday, we go around and share one thing that we are thankful for that week. When I first introduce this to students, most answers are vague. As the year goes on, it is clear that students are more thoughtful about their answers. They are truly realizing both big and small ways that they are grateful! It's heartwarming to see this growth throughout the year.

I believe that the environment around you can greatly impact your mood, presence, and attitude. I work hard to ensure that my classroom environment and home space reflect calmness, comfort, and purpose. In my classroom, I use soft lighting and comfortable seating, and am cautious not to overstimulate my students with posters and work covering the walls. I believe that students are more calm and focused in an environment that is just that. I enjoy simple decorations and blank spaces on my walls! Of course, I like to hang up student work and anchor charts. However, I am more thoughtful about what goes on my walls. This way, anything that is displayed has a purpose and isn't just there to take up space. I carry this over to my home as well. I enjoy simple spaces with cozy touches, such as throw blankets, plants, and dimmed lighting.

MINIMIZING PHONE TIME

I have really become more conscious of the time I spend on my phone, especially on social media. I utilize the "screen time" feature on my iPhone, that tracks how much time you are on your phone. It even breaks it up into time spent on social media, games, health and fitness, etc. I limit myself to two hours a day! I have my phone set to lock me out of my social media apps after two hours. At first, this was extremely difficult! I would suggest using the screen time feature to determine how much time you spend on your phone on average in a day. Then, make a goal from there! Maybe start at one hour less each day. When you're spending less time on your phone, you give more quality time and energy to your environment and the people in your environment!

SUPPORT FOR THE "GRATEFUL MINIMALISM" JOURNEY

I am inspired by many others who are on their gratitude and minimalism journeys! I absolutely love the *Simply Grateful* gratitude journal from Target! It can be found in the "gift" aisle, next to party favors and gift bags. It has so many thoughtful prompts and quotes.

My favorite Instagram accounts to follow for inspiration are: @beginathome; @houseofeilers; @minimalist.motherhood; @letsliveandlearn; @thesimplifiedmom; and of course, you can follow me at @simply__grateful

> THE SECRET OF HAPPINESS, YOU SEE, IS NOT FOUND IN SEEKING MORE, BUT IN DEVELOPING THE CAPACITY TO ENJOY LESS. >> SOCRATES

your guide to planning classroom PARTIES

BY SHANNON GAREAU

As teachers, we inevitably become master multitaskers! In the classroom, teaching content is just one of the many hats we wear throughout any given day. Some of those hats include counselor, nurse, comedian, detective, janitor, mentor, and party planner!

When I first began my teaching career, planning a classroom party, amidst all the other daily tasks, seemed trivial. However, when I actually set out to plan my first classroom Halloween party, it ended up costing me a great deal of time, stress, money, and anxiety. With all the other roles and responsibilities that come with teaching, classroom party planning shouldn't become one more dreaded task. The organizational tips I've discovered throughout my years of teaching will help you eliminate some of the stress and make your next classroom party enjoyable for both you and your students.

This guide to planning classroom parties will break down these organizational tips and help make your next classroom party a stress-free success!

Keep It Simple
You know what they say; "less is more!" This rule definitely applies when planning a classroom party. This organizational tip may seem fairly obvious, but in the age of Pinterest, it is really easy to get carried away with thousands of ideas at your fingertips. With so much inspiration out there, if you're like me, you may find yourself getting overwhelmed with so many options. In my experience, most kids appreciate simplicity when it comes to a classroom party. Too many decorations, too much junk food, and too many activities leave kids (as well as teachers and parents) feeling overstimulated and crabby. Instead of trying to do a lot of different activities, pick a few things to plan really well.

For older students, give a choice or let them vote on what to do during the party. Most older kids just appreciate a break in the routine of the school day and a chance to socialize with their peers. They aren't looking for a super structured class party, and sometimes just watching a movie together is exciting for them. Instead of stressing yourself out with planning every detail, give older students a chance to give input and they will appreciate the time even more. Keeping the decorations, food, and activities simple for class parties has tremendous benefits for everyone involved.

Plan Ahead
As teachers, we know the importance of planning in advance. Planning a classroom party is no different. Before the school year starts, check with the office about what parties you are able to have and when they can be held throughout the year. Get them on your school's calendar as soon as possible and start planning them in advance. Giving parents plenty of notice about upcoming events gives them ample time to sign up to help and to send in party supplies. Along with parents having a heads up, students will be motivated and look forward to the event once it's on the calendar. Many teachers put out sign-up sheets during Parent Night to get volunteers and generate interest for upcoming parties and events.

Find a Focus
As a teacher, it is ingrained in our brains to plan with a purpose. All of our lessons have a clear objective and focus, so why wouldn't we plan our classroom parties in a similar way? Now, I know what you're thinking: parties are supposed to be fun, not standardized, and I totally agree! However, after years of planning classroom parties, I've realized that having a focus or theme makes it a lot less chaotic and a lot more fun for everyone involved.

When planning a party, it's helpful to think about the message we are sending our students. Do we want them to view class parties as major pig-out sessions where we embrace chaos and waste food? Or do we want them to view class parties as fun times spent with classmates, making memories? When I had my first classroom party, I definitely had no focus or theme whatsoever. That lack of focus resulted in copious amounts of junk food, a ton of leftover waste, and kids that could care less about any of the other activities because they had eaten too much sugar.

After that, I came across an idea in an article called *A New Kind of Class Party* by Teacher Trap. I loved the idea that "a class party should be about celebrating and making memories together, not just eating junk food together. Kids don't need the junk food to have fun. Kids just want to do something out of the ordinary and to connect with both their teacher and classmates in a new way!" The author went on to explain that by putting a focus on purpose, a focus on making memories, and a focus on novelty, you can transform your class party into a wonderful experience for everyone involved.

Ask For Help
As a new teacher, I was afraid to ask for help. I felt

easy games & activities

Stacking Cup Game
For this party game, all you need is a timer and plastic cups. First, split the cups into 2 groups, and have two kids compete against each other. The students have to unstack the cups, create a pyramid, and then restack the cups back into each other. Use the timer to keep track of the time it takes them to accomplish this. The student who does this the fastest wins! You can do this with any number of cups you would like, but I've always used 21 cups to make a pyramid with a 6-cup base. If you want to have more than 2 kids compete at a time, just add more cups. If you don't want to keep track of the time, you could also do this activity more like a relay race.

Free Printables
Pinterest has a plethora of free printables for any classroom theme party! I've found great resources that include holiday puzzles, word searches, and coloring contest pages that the students really seem to enjoy working on. A few of these resources are great to have on hand in case there's any down-time during a classroom party or if your activities end ahead of schedule.

like I was "bothering" parents or coworkers, and didn't want to cause stress for anyone else. Looking back, I realize how ridiculous and unrealistic that was! If I could go back and tell my "new teacher self" anything, it would be this: Don't be afraid to ask for help.

One of the reasons my first classroom party was such a disaster was because I tried to do everything by myself. From the decorations to the activities, and even some of the goodies, I was on my own. I spent way too much money and time planning the party, and in the end it wasn't even that successful, and it left me feeling stressed and exhausted.

Throughout my years of teaching I've realized that parents love to help and come into the classroom, so now I embrace it! I now believe that the teacher should set the focus and expectations of the party, but then delegate, delegate, delegate! Make a list of everything that is needed for the party and be as specific as possible. Then parents can sign up for whatever they would like to bring or do. Parents are more willing to help out with a party if the expectations are communicated clearly and they know exactly what is needed from them.

Creating a signup sheet for open house is a great way to generate interest and gather parent contact information. Once you have the parents' information, using an app such as *SignUpGenius* or *SignUp.com* can help organize and delegate responsibilities with ease. This saves so much time. Instead of tracking everyone down based on a paper sign up sheet, you just make a list of everything needed and then allow parents to sign up to do their part. Automated reminders help ensure no one forgets. Free online aids like this help make party planning and delegating run more smoothly with less effort on the teacher's part.

When creating your signup sheet or list, it's important to be specific and cover all areas of the party. An article on *Upper Elementary Snapshots* came in handy for me by suggesting some important areas to remember when asking for help.

These areas include: setting up, running the party, taking party photos, cleaning up, decorating, sending in paper goods, providing crafts or game supplies, creating goodie bags, and bringing healthy snacks. Providing parents with tasks and ways to help will ensure better communication. Better communication will ultimately make parents more eager and willing to help out in the classroom, even if they are not able to make it the day of the party.

Stick to a Schedule

The word schedule doesn't exactly scream party or fun, but sticking to a (flexible) schedule will save your sanity during your next class party. Breaking down your allotted time into five or ten minute increments will help kids and parent volunteers transition more easily from one activity to the next. Have an agenda on hand, but remember that a game may take less time than expected, and snacks and treats may expand into a longer time slot than you expected as students socialize. As teachers, lesson planning is a must, and helps daily activities run smoothly in the classroom. Making a flexible schedule for the party helps teachers, parents and students know what to expect, stay on track, and ultimately have more fun!

Plan a Menu

When planning a class party, it's important to first check for allergies or school regulations. You don't want to leave a child out or cause a problem on party day. Once you know what you can or cannot have at the party, then start asking parents for help with the menu. Be specific when asking parents to sign up for food items. Ask for a mix of healthy treats and sweets so that you don't end up with a ton of sugar or a ton of leftovers. The first organizational tip of "Keep It Simple" definitely applies when planning a menu. Too much food, especially junk food, is not necessary and can be wasteful.

Another important tip when planning a menu is to make sure the parent that brings each food item also brings serving utensils for it. I can't tell you how many times parents have brought in these amazing dishes, but then forget to bring something to put them in or some way to serve them. It's always nerve-racking to be scrambling during the party to find something to cut the cake or scoop the ice cream while the kids lose patience because they want to get their hands on the delicious treat.

The best food items are already portioned (individual serving sizes or put into bags) and ready to be passed out, without any interruption to the party. I've also observed that kids are more likely to choose healthy alternatives, like fruit, when it is already cut up and portioned out for them. Specify this prep in your sign-up sheet so you don't end up with a full pineapple or an uncut watermelon.

The phrase "classroom party" should not cause stress and anxiety to an already overworked classroom teacher. Following these organizational tips should help alleviate some of that stress and help get the ball rolling for your next classroom party.

We all know how much our students look forward to classroom parties. Wouldn't it be nice if teachers looked forward to them as well? Classroom parties should be fun, relatively easy, and stress-free. Focusing on simplicity, and planning will make your next classroom party a stress-free, enjoyable experience for all party participants!

healthy snack options

Cut-Up Fruit
Kids love bite-sized, easy to eat treats! When fruit is cut up, kids are much more likely to put it on their plates and actually eat it. Apple slices, grapes, small clementines, cut-up watermelon, and bananas are some classroom party favorites. Fruit is a great alternative to other sugar-laden foods because of its sweet taste. Adding a fruit dip on the side makes this healthier snack option even more enticing for kids.

Popcorn and Chex Mix or Trail Mix
Popcorn is a kid party favorite! It's a more nutritious choice than chips because it offers a little bit of fiber. It's also easy to make and easy to serve at a classroom party. Trail mix also falls into this healthier category, and gives students more variety.

Sandwich Pops
Sandwich Pops are so adorable and fun to eat! An article titled "10 Healthy Kid's Birthday Party Snacks" on evite.com describes Sandwich Pops as "another fun way to enjoy a protein paired with a colorful fruit or veggie. Serve a combo of grapes, cheese and whole grain crusty bread cubes on small skewers for bite-size snacks." Kids can enjoy this healthy deconstructed sandwich, and fill up on protein and veggies, instead of candy and sugar.

Printable Labels
Adding some flair to bottles of water, juice boxes, or kid-friendly snacks with a cute label can go a long way! You can find adorable low-cost or free printable tags online that go along with your classroom party theme. Pinterest has so many creative ideas to choose from. Adding a "Melted Snowman" label to a bottle of water makes a Winter holiday party more festive. Putting pipe cleaners, googly eyes, and a red pom pom on any packaged snack gives you an instant reindeer. A cheesecloth will turn any drink into a mummy! The options are endless, and you can really be crafty by customizing the accessories to fit your class party theme!

Heads or Tails
This game is so easy to play, and a big hit with students! All you need to play is a coin and Mardi Gras beads, three per student. I got my beads from the Dollar Tree. Each student is given 3 necklaces to wear at the beginning of the game. They must decide if they think the flipped coin will be head or tails before the coin is flipped. If they choose heads, they face the front of the room, and put their hands on their head. If they choose tails, they turn around and put their hands on their "tail," or hips. After everyone has made their decision, the coin is flipped, and the winning side is announced. If the student was incorrect with their choice, they must take off one of their strings of beads. Once a student loses all 3 of their necklaces, they are out of the game. The game is played until only one student is remaining.

Bingo
Bingo is always a classroom favorite. There are plenty of free bingo printables online. You can find generic printables that can be used for any type of classroom party, or more specific printables depending on the theme or season. You can also spice up the game of Bingo by using different "markers" depending on the theme. For example, use candy corn for Halloween, kisses or candy hearts for Valentine's Day, or even fun highlighters to make the game more exciting for the students.

5 Ways to Style a MONOCHROMATIC OUTFIT

CARMEN MYER @THEGOODCARMABLOG

As we all know by the return of scrunchies, mom jeans, and chokers, fashion trends come and go. I am not one to invest in a trend but instead I look at my closet and see how I can utilize what I already have. One trend I fell in love with while scrolling through magazines is monochromatic fashion. I was drawn to the outfits made up of winter whites or different shades of green. I challenged myself to use my own closet to recreate these high fashion looks in a way that was more suited for my lifestyle. While winter whites and 5 inch heels are beautiful, I'm not wearing them around my preschool and kindergarten students. This challenge for me was a good way to refresh my closet and use items that have been forgotten. Next time I'm feeling this itch to have an ASOS or Nordstrom shopping spree, I'll do this instead. Here are a few easy monochromatic looks I created with items I already owned. I hope you enjoy trying them!

Grey All Day

This all grey outfit was a little bit out of my comfort zone because I usually enjoy more form fitting outfits. I paired an oversized grey jumpsuit with a long grey duster for this outfit and ended up really enjoying wearing it. The different tones of grey and the different fabrics made this the perfect monochromatic outfit.

Loungewear (a.k.a. Fancy Pajamas)

After being home for over a month during the end of the school year, I am sure we all have a plethora of loungewear in our dresser drawers. I paired mauve leggings with a bubblegum pink sweater for this lazy Sunday look. Cheers to looking like our cutest selves even when we're at home binge-watching Netflix's latest kooky documentary.

Double Denim

I remember the first time hearing the term double denim when I wore a denim dress and jean jacket to a school dance. Supposedly, it was a fashion no-no, but I have been a double denim enthusiast ever since! The key is to make sure your denim isn't too matchy-matchy. I paired a dark blue denim jean with a sky blue top and medium wash jean jacket to get the perfect blend of denim.

4 The perfect night out look: a simple top and skirt combination, but in an amazing color! This peach bodysuit and skirt are both items I typically do not wear often but have since been moved to the front of their rightful sections in my closet after putting together this bright and fun look!

Peachy ~ Keen!

5 I tend to gravitate towards wearing bright or muted colors on a daily basis, but always reach for my black items when I cannot figure out what to wear. Black makes every outfit feel more elevated and helps you to look put together even when you may not feel that way. To make this all black outfit a little bit more interesting, I added a top and shoes with prints on them to draw the eye up and down.

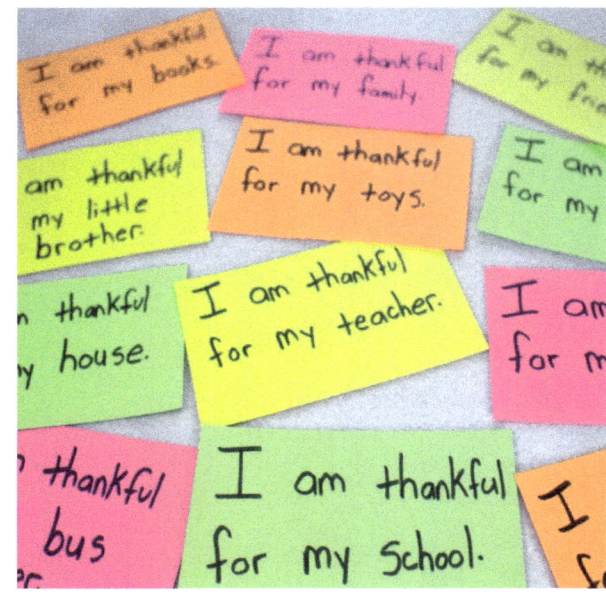
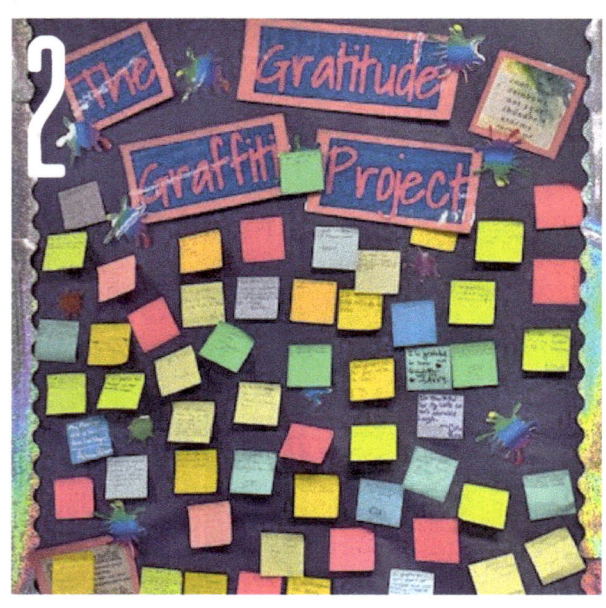

GROWING IN GRATITUDE

1 @CARLYANDADAM

Reinforce a mindful approach to gratitude by having students create gratitude towers. For this fun, hands-on STEM activity, students are given a pile of index cards. On each card, they write one thing they are thankful for. Using their index cards and tape, students work in small groups to create the tallest tower. The more things they are thankful for, the bigger the tower will be! For more hands-on STEM challenge ideas, check out our blog. www.carlyandadam.com

2 @TEACHINGSPARKLES

My 6th grade students love sharing their gratitude! Every night they write down 3 things they are grateful for from that day. On Fridays, they choose one piece of gratitude to share, and then add it to our Gratitude board to display for the week!

3 @BEWELLINSCHOOL

We create notebooks with students for them to use as gratitude journals and as a place to keep track of self-regulation strategies that work for them. We work with students to help them see that practicing gratitude is a strategy! Research shows that practicing daily gratitude leads to better physical and mental health, improved sleep, deeper relationships, and a stronger sense of self-esteem. We believe that an integral part of gratitude is being grateful for who we are, what we are, and all that we can do by simply existing. Waking up each morning and having the opportunity to begin again is reason enough to be grateful!

4 @FEEDTHEBIRDIES

Our campus taught gratitude in our Connections (home room) classes, and we usually create gratitude trees and write our notes on leaves to attach. This year, I decided that I wanted my students to see how practicing gratitude daily and making it a habit would change their whole perspective on so many levels. I put together small stacks of paper to create junk journals with my kids that they could keep with them to reflect on. They each chose their papers and then we put them together, and put an actual leaf to press in an envelope in the journal to remind us of this season in our lives. The students really liked the thoughtfulness and personalization of the journal.

> THE SECRET TO HAVING IT ALL IS KNOWING THAT YOU ALREADY DO.

WHAT TO DO WHEN
GRATITUDE ELUDES YOU

It's not always sunny inside a teacher's mind. Some days, you know that you should be practicing gratitude, and *want* to take steps to acheive greater happiness, but you just can't seem to force that feeling. **What if you're having trouble connecting with gratitude right now, in your current season of life?**

These small tips, tweaks, and thought reversals may help get you reconnected with your grateful spirit.

Language Adjustments
Frame a feeling with terminology that leads you to direct your gratitude to the right source. Instead of "I'm so lucky," make a habit of starting to say "I'm so blessed." This subtle language shift will lead to a greater mindset shift.

Self Perception
Self esteem / awareness is interwoven with gratitude. Start at the center of your being. What part of yourself are you most grateful for? Internalize the feelings of thankfulness and connect them with your own soul.

Basic Needs
Even when you may feel that you don't have a lot to be grateful for, you can consciously seek out elements that you do have. Focus on searching for parts of your life where you have "stability," "enoughness," or "peace." Zero in on those aspects, the ones you tend to generally take for granted. Where you find that feeling of stability or feel that you have "enough" is where your thankful habits can begin.

Awareness
Are you so deep inside your own bubble that you can't see clearly? Sometimes a splash of perspective is all it takes. Instead of comparing yourself to people who may appear to have it all, reflect on someone who you would never want to trade places with. Suddenly, your perspective may shift to help you feel grateful for what you do have.

Start with People
Go outside of yourself, and think of a human who you are grateful to have in your life. Go actively show that person how you feel. Passing gratitude on in a visible way can encourage it to grow inside your own heart.

Stories
Which type of story makes you feel more grateful, a happy one, or a sad one? Do you feel grateful for your own health when you see a child with cancer? Or for your own country when you see the horrors of genocide and terrorism across the world? For some people, this can lead to a grateful spark. For others, a happy story does the trick. Do you feel grateful for the gift of life when you see a story of a community coming together to help a neighbor in need? Start noticing any gratitude that flows from each story that you hear. Allow these outside situations to light up your own grateful feelings.

Teach It
Get yourself started on a journey of finding gratitude by teaching someone else how. We know as teachers that you learn and make a habit of something most easily by teaching it! If you begin phrasing what you say in a way that teaches grateful habits, you'll start to soak them up for yourself as well. Guide your students to note their grateful experiences, and you'll naturally start spotting your own. The Law of Attraction applies here. Focusing on something brings it into reality.

Practice Makes Ease
Gratitude is not automatic. That's why we call it "practicing" gratitude. It takes work.

Don't Fear the Negative
Be aware that true, deep happiness that springs up from a grateful attitude must stem from an awareness of the bad. You can't fully embrace joy as an adult without understanding sadness and having that contrast. Gratitude for the good parts of your life does not require you to ignore the negativity, the depression, the stress, or the sadness. In fact, those down-moments become the comparison you use to see the joys. If you are in a moment of pain right now, and struggling with finding a grateful stance, you'll someday use that as a reference point that brings your contentment down the road to an even higher level.

Cycle Up
Outlook can be cyclical. Those who start spiraling upward with a grateful attitude tend to keep on going, while those who neglect to focus on being grateful will often continue on a downward spiral. Choose your habits with intentionality.

What if you woke up tomorrow with only the things you thanked God for today?

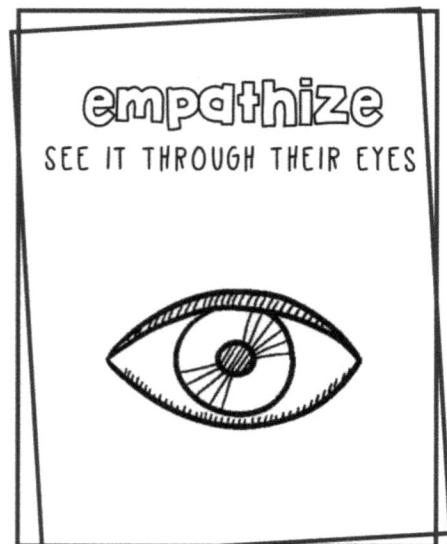

empathize
SEE IT THROUGH THEIR EYES

choose right
DO THE TOUGH THING

be a friend
WHEN THEY NEED IT, NOT ONLY WHEN YOU NEED IT

be brave
STAND UP FOR SELF & OTHERS

serve
GIVE TO OTHERS

build peace
BE A CONFLICT SOLVER

character traits & kindness

show respect — TREAT OTHERS AS YOU'D LIKE TO BE TREATED

contribute — MAKE YOUR COMMUNITY BETTER

reach out — WHO NEEDS YOU TODAY?

be honest — BE KNOWN FOR TRUTHFULNESS

spread joy — A CHEERFUL ATTITUDE IS PROVEN TO BE CONTAGIOUS!

be responsible — FOR ACTIONS, ENVIRONMENT, AND RULES

guard your thoughts — THEY BECOME ACTIONS

Inspiration from...

C. S. LEWIS

The task of the modern educator is not to cut down jungles but to irrigate deserts.

We do not want merely to see beauty ... We want something else which can hardly be put into words — to be united with the beauty we see, to pass into it, to receive it into ourselves, to bathe in it, to become part of it.

What you see and what you hear depends a great deal on where you are standing. It also depends on what sort of person you are.

Miracles are a retelling in small letters of the very same story which is written across the whole world in letters too large for some of us to see.

When we lose one blessing, another is often most unexpectedly given in its place.

Isn't it funny how day by day nothing changes, but when you look back, everything is different ...

Forgiveness does not mean excusing.

Thirst was made for water; inquiry for truth.

The truth is, of course, that what one regards as interruptions are precisely one's life.

Love is something more stern and splendid than mere kindness.

Aim at heaven and you will get earth thrown in. Aim at earth and you get neither.

Quotes from C.S. Lewis

www.ingramcontent.com/pod-product-compliance
Lightning Source LLC
Chambersburg PA
CBHW042038100526
44587CB00030B/4477